New York State ELA

English Language Arts

W9-AGJ-047

Continental Press

Credits

Editorial Development: Beth Spencer, Jane Nicholas

Cover Design: Kay Walker

Interior Design: Crystal Crater

Illustrators: Pages 27, 49, 55, 103, 108, 109, 112, 114, 118, 122, 124, 127, 130, 135, 139, 144, 158, 165, 167, 169, 172, 180, 190, 194, Laurie Conley; Pages 30, 37, 52, 105, 116, 120, 154, 164, 171, 177, 178, 183, 184, 189, Michael Fink; Pages 58, 99, 141, Dave Stirba

Photo Credits: Front cover and title page: *Boldt Castle,* Daniel Boyce, www.northernphotography.com; Page 26 *supermarket,* www.istockphoto.com/lisegagne; Page 34 *Shirley Chisholm,* Library of Congress, Prints and Photographs Division, LC-USZ62-83472; Page 40 *pronghorn,* www.istockphoto.com/yoshimedia; Page 47 *octopus,* www.istockphoto.com/DanSchmitt; Page 56 courtesy of USFWS; Page 60 *Fort Ticonderoga,* AP Photo/Jim McKnight; Page 67 courtesy of NASA/JPL; Page 81 *schoolroom,* www.istockphoto.com/joaofilipe; Page 83 *Mohawk Trail Highway,* AP Photo/Nancy Palmieri; Page 85 *Blizzard of '88,* NOAA/Historic NWS Collection; Page 88 courtesy of www.marssociety.org; Page 91 *starling,* www.istockphoto.com/johncl; Page 94 *Brooklyn Bridge,* www.istockphoto.com/Steve; Page 175 *Iroquois longhouse,* courtesy of http://american-native-art.com/publication/iroquois/foto; Page 181 *firefighters,* www.istockphoto.com/mrorange002; Page 184 *hawks,* AP Photo/Lincoln Karim; Page 187 *Niagara Falls,* www.photos.com

ISBN 978-0-8454-4929-5

Contents

Introduction to New York State English Language Arts Grade 4 4

Unit 1: Vocabulary Strategies [Literacy Competencies] 5
   Lesson 1 Word Parts 6
   Lesson 2 Words in Context 16

Unit 2: Reading and Writing for Information [Standard 1] 25
   Lesson 3 Organizational Features 26
   Lesson 4 Finding the Sequence 33
   Lesson 5 Prior Knowledge 40
   Lesson 6 Main Idea and Details 47
   Lesson 7 Cause and Effect 55
   Lesson 8 Comparison and Contrast 63
   Lesson 9 The Writing Process 69
   Lesson 10 Editing a Paragraph 80
   Lesson 11 Writing a Short Response 84
   Lesson 12 Writing an Extended Response 90

Unit 3: Reading and Writing with Literature [Standard 2] 97
   Lesson 13 Story Elements 98
   Lesson 14 Story Structure 108
   Lesson 15 Making Reading Connections 114
   Lesson 16 Making Predictions 120
   Lesson 17 Inferences and Conclusions 126
   Lesson 18 Figurative Language 132
   Lesson 19 Poetry and Plays 138
   Lesson 20 Writing About Literature 151

Unit 4: Reading and Writing for Critical Analysis [Standard 3] 163
   Lesson 21 Author's Purpose 164
   Lesson 22 Fact and Opinion 171
   Lesson 23 Analyzing Ideas 177
   Lesson 24 Making Judgments 183
   Lesson 25 Writing to Analyze 189

Welcome to English Language Arts!

Everyone wants to do well on tests. Tests help your teacher and school see the progress you are making, and they help you get ready for the next step in your education. This book was written to help you get ready for the *New York State English Language Arts Test*. On the test you will read fiction and nonfiction selections and answer multiple-choice questions about them. You will also listen as your teacher reads a selection. And you will write answers, called *short responses* and *extended responses*.

The lessons in this book will help you improve your skills in vocabulary, reading, and writing. You will read nonfiction articles as well as stories, poems, and plays. As you answer questions, you will learn how to plan and write a good answer. You will also learn ways to examine selections to decide if they are true and complete. Then you will write your own analysis of the selections and the ideas in them. You will use all of these skills when you take the test.

The reading and writing lessons in this book are in three parts.

- The first part of the lesson introduces the reading or writing skill you are going to study and explains what it is and how you use it.

- The second part is called Guided Practice. You will get more than just practice here, you will get help. You will read a selection and answer questions. After each question you will find an explanation of the correct answer. So you will answer questions and find out right away if you are right. You will also learn *why* one answer is right and the others are not.

- The third part is called Test Yourself. This time you will read a selection and answer the questions on your own.

You will answer multiple-choice questions and you will write some answers.

Now you are ready to use this book. When you finish, you'll be ready for the New York State test. Good luck!

Unit 1: Vocabulary Strategies

When you read, it's important to understand the meaning of words so that you can make sense of what you read. Understanding vocabulary will help you in all the reading that you do. It will also help you answer questions on tests. On a test, you may be asked what a word or phrase means. If you know the word or phrase, it will be easy to answer the question. But if you're not sure of the meaning, you need to find another way to answer the question. As you work through this unit, you will learn ways to find the meaning of words you don't know.

There are two lessons in this unit:

1 **Word Parts** includes prefixes, suffixes, base words, and compound words. You can use your knowledge of these word parts to figure out the meaning of a word on a test.

2 **Words in Context** shows you how to use information in a reading selection to figure out the meaning of a word you don't know. You will also learn about idioms—phrases that have different meanings from the actual words.

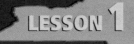

Prefixes, Suffixes, and Base Words

Many words are made up of different parts. A word may have a **prefix,** a **base word,** and a **suffix.** If you know what some or all of the parts mean, you can figure out the meaning of the word.

un-   friend   -ly

friend is the base word

un- is a prefix that means "not"   **-ly** is a suffix that means "like"

So, the word <u>unfriendly</u> means "not acting like a friend."

Prefixes

A **prefix** is a word part added to the beginning of the word. A prefix changes the meaning of the base word to make a new word. The prefix *un-* means "not." If you add *un-* to the word <u>happy</u>, you make a new word that means "not happy."

Prefix Chart

Prefix	Meaning	Example
in-	in, not	<u>in</u>dependent
over-	too much, too long	<u>over</u>done
pre-	before	<u>pre</u>package
re-	back, again	<u>re</u>play
sub-	under	<u>sub</u>marine
super-	over, higher, bigger	<u>super</u>market
un-	not	<u>un</u>pleasant
under-	below, not up to	<u>under</u>shirt

Match a prefix with each of these base words to make a word that fits the new meaning.

PREFIX	BASE WORD	NEW MEANING
	record	before making a record
	use	use too much
	ground	below the ground
	able	not able to do
	visit	visit again

Guided Practice

Answer the following questions.

The word <u>incorrect</u> means

A probably right

B right again

C always right

D not right

> Look back at the chart. The prefix *in-* means "not." The base word *correct* means "right." So <u>incorrect</u> means "not correct" or "not right." D is the correct answer.

The word <u>prepaid</u> means

A paid ahead of time

B paid too late

C not paid

D prepared for

> Since the prefix *pre-* means "before," and "ahead of time" means the same thing, the answer must be A.

The word <u>overdue</u> means

A tired

B late

C above

D ready

> The correct answer is B. You know that the prefix *over-* means "too much" or "too long." Something that is <u>overdue</u> has been due too long.

Suffixes

A **suffix** is a word part added to the end of the word. A suffix also changes the meaning of a word.

> Your friendship means a lot to me.

You know what *friend* means. The suffix *-ship* means "the quality or state of something." Friendship is the state of being friends.

Some suffixes change words to different parts of speech. When you add the suffix *-ly* to the noun *friend*, you make the word *friendly*, which is an adjective.

Suffix Chart

Suffix	Meaning	Example
-able	able to	breakable
-er	one who does something	painter
-ful	full of, likely to	restful
-ish	being like	childish
-less	without	homeless
-ly	like, in that way	perfectly
-ness	quality or state of	goodness
-ship	quality or state of	citizenship

Match a suffix with each of these words to make a word that fits the new meaning.

WORD	SUFFIX	NEW MEANING	NEW WORD
care		without taking care	
thank		full of thanks	
train		one who trains people or animals	
citizen		state of being a citizen	
dark		state of being dark	

Guided Practice

Answer the following questions.

The word <u>chewable</u> describes

    A   something that has been chewed

    B   the act of chewing something

    C   something that can be chewed

    D   a part of a dog's chew toy

> The clue to the answer is the suffix *-able*. Just like the word *able*, the suffix means "able to be" or "can." The clue tells you that the correct answer is C.

The word <u>lateness</u> means

    A   likely to be late

    B   like someone who is late

    C   not being late

    D   the state of being late

> The suffix *-ness* means "quality or state of." Try to use the word in a sentence. (Rob got a warning for his <u>lateness</u>.) The answer is D.

The word <u>babyish</u> means

    A   like a baby

    B   a person who babies others

    C   near a baby

    D   a person who has no baby

> Since the suffix *-ish* means "being like," <u>babyish</u> must mean "being like a baby." The correct answer is A.

Base Words

Prefixes and suffixes must be added to **base words.** If you know what the base word means and you know what different prefixes and suffixes mean, you can often figure out the meaning of new words. Remember this word?

un-   friend   -ly

friend is the base word

un- is a prefix that means "not"   **-ly** is a suffix that means "like"

Here is a web of words with the base word <u>do</u>.

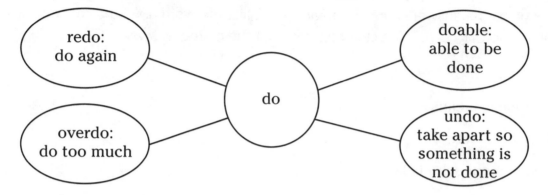

Choose the correct word from the web for each sentence below.

1   Don't _____ the gardening or you will be tired.

2   Rhan thinks the project is _____ in ten days.

3   I will have to _____ the homework I lost.

4   Can you _____ the knot you tied?

Guided Practice

Answer the following questions.

What is the base word of <u>unkindness</u>?

    A unkind

    B kind

    C kindness

    D kindly

Write the meaning of <u>unkindness</u>.

_____

_____

> You know that *un-* is a prefix and *-ness* is a suffix. If you take them away, the base word is left. So the correct answer is *kind,* choice B. <u>Unkindness</u> means "the quality or state of not being kind."

What is the base word of <u>repayable</u>?

    A pay

    B repay

    C payable

    D paying

Write the meaning of <u>repayable</u>.

_____

_____

> Without the prefix *re-* and the suffix *-able,* you have the base word *pay.* The correct answer is A. <u>Repayable</u> means "able to be paid back."

Compound Words

A **compound word** is made up of two smaller words. The words that make up a compound word can stand alone, unlike prefixes or suffixes.

You can make several compound words with the word *sea*: *seashore, seafood, seashell, seaweed,* and *seagull*. If you don't know what a compound word means, you can try to figure out its meaning from the words that make up the compound word.

Here are some compound words that you probably know.

WORD		WORD		COMPOUND WORD
bath	+	room	=	bathroom
air	+	port	=	airport
camp	+	fire	=	campfire
high	+	way	=	highway
girl	+	friend	=	girlfriend

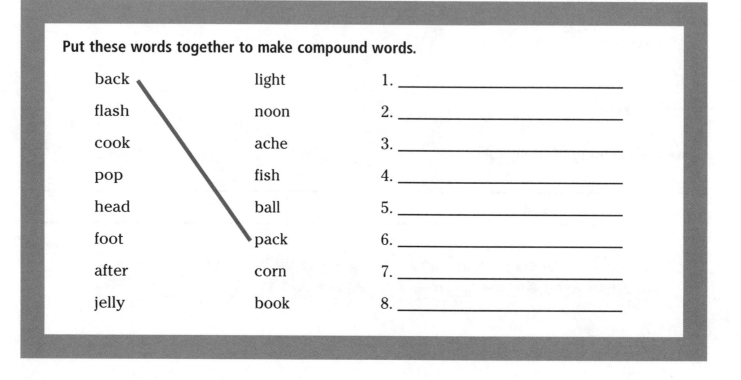

Put these words together to make compound words.

back	light	1. _____
flash	noon	2. _____
cook	ache	3. _____
pop	fish	4. _____
head	ball	5. _____
foot	pack	6. _____
after	corn	7. _____
jelly	book	8. _____

Guided Practice

Read the following selection and answer the questions that follow.

Our backyard is just about big enough for a ball field. A group of us kids play softball there after school. We use old sweatshirts for the bases, but we have a good softball and bat. We don't have enough people for a real team, so everybody plays a couple of positions. Usually we have just one person in the outfield.

A <u>backyard</u> is _____ a house.

A	next to	**C**	behind
B	in front of	**D**	inside

Look for a word that is related to one of the words that make up <u>backyard</u>. *Back* and *behind* mean about the same thing. Choice C is the correct answer.

A <u>sweatshirt</u> is

A	something to wear	**C**	a soft pillow
B	something to sit on	**D**	a big towel

The clue in the word <u>sweatshirt</u> is the word *shirt*. You know that a shirt is something to wear. That tells you that a <u>sweatshirt</u> is something to wear, too. So the correct choice is A.

The <u>outfield</u> is

A	near the house	**C**	next to the garage
B	close to home plate	**D**	away from the bases

Both parts of the word <u>outfield</u> help you understand its meaning. In a ball park, the <u>outfield</u> is out in a field. That means it is away from the bases, choice D.

Test Yourself

Read the following selection and answer the questions that follow.

People aren't the only creatures who use ladders. Some salmon do, too. These fish live in the sea, but in the spring they swim up large streams and rivers. The salmon travel to small, quiet streams where they lay their eggs. Just any quiet stream won't do. Salmon like to lay their eggs in the same stream where they were born.

Streams and rivers often have waterfalls. Salmon can leap as high as 10 feet to get over these falls on their way upstream. Yet now, dams have been built to block many waterways. Some of them stand 50 feet or higher. That's too high even for these champion jumpers.

The builders had to rethink the design of the dams. They decided to build "ladders" into the dams. A fish ladder looks like a stairway filled with water. Each concrete step has a pool and is about a foot higher than the one below it. The ladder is specially built so that the water flows slowly down the steps. The salmon jump from step to step. If they get overtired, they can swim around for a while in large resting pools.

1 A <u>stairway</u> usually connects

   A pools of water

   B rivers and streams

   C rooms in a building

   D floors in a building

2 The word <u>specially</u> means

    A for a special person

    B in a special way

    C in a special place

    D with special tools

3 In this selection, the word <u>jumper</u> means

    A a fish that can jump

    B something to jump over

    C a very high cliff

    D a way to start a car

4 To <u>rethink</u> means to

    A think about

    B not think

    C think again

    D stop thinking

5 A <u>waterfall</u> is

    A a ladder for salmon to climb

    B a place where water falls over a cliff

    C a place for water sports

    D a dam built to keep fish away from streams

6 The word <u>overtired</u> means

    A lost

    B not tired

    C too tired

    D asleep

Words in Context

Your vocabulary is made up of all the words you know. You use many words to speak and write. But you know even more words than the ones you use. They are the words you understand when you listen or read.

When you read, you probably don't know every word you see. You can often figure out the meaning of a new word from other words near it. These are called **context clues.**

Read this sentence from *Charlotte's Web.*

One afternoon, she heard a most interesting conversation and witnessed a strange event.

You may know that the word witnessed means "saw." If you didn't know the word, you could figure out its meaning from other words and ideas in the sentence. Charlotte *heard* something first—a conversation. What goes with hearing something? Seeing something. So, witnessed probably means "saw." The word *event* gives you another clue. You wouldn't just hear an event, you would watch it, too.

You can look for specific types of context clues when you read. Here are four kinds: **synonyms, examples, definitions,** and **descriptions.**

Type of context clue	Synonyms	Examples	Definitions	Descriptions
What they do	have nearly the same meaning	show what a word means	tell what a word means	tell more about a word

Unit 1 Vocabulary Strategies

Synonyms

A sentence or paragraph might use two synonyms, or words that have meanings that are nearly the same. If you know the meaning of one word, you can figure out the meaning of the other.

> The pages of the old book were <u>tattered</u> and <u>torn</u>.

The words <u>tattered</u> and <u>torn</u> both tell about an old book. Even if you didn't know the meaning of <u>tattered</u>, you could figure it out. In this sentence, <u>tattered</u> means about the same as <u>torn</u>, or "in pieces or rags." <u>Tattered</u> and <u>torn</u> are synonyms.

Examples

Some sentences or paragraphs give examples to show what a word means. Look at the word <u>groom</u> in the first sentence below. Can you figure out what it means from the sentence that follows?

> It was Jenna's turn to <u>groom</u> Peaches, the family dog. She got out the wire brush and started to work on Peaches' long silky fur.

What does the word <u>groom</u> mean? You might think it means walk. But the example shows that Jenna is using a brush on the dog's fur. So <u>groom</u> probably means "to brush and clean."

Definitions

Definitions are another kind of context clue. Look for the definition in this sentence:

> We climbed up the <u>embankment</u>, a tangle of roots and weeds sloping away from the road.

An <u>embankment</u> is a small hill or slope by the side of a road or a body of water. The words in the sentence after <u>embankment</u> give you a definition. The word *climb* is another clue that an <u>embankment</u> is a hill.

Descriptions

Sometimes a sentence will have a description that tells you what a word means. Do you see the description in this sentence?

> Jason walked down the long hall of the dormitory, looking into the students' bedrooms on either side.

You may not know what a dormitory is, but you can figure out its meaning from the sentence. The sentence tells you that it has a hall, so it must be a building. Then the sentence describes part of the building: on either side of the hall, there are bedrooms for students. So, a dormitory is a building where students live.

Guided Practice

Read the following selection and answer the questions that follow.

Webs aren't the only things for which spiders use their special silk. The silk is important for newborn spiders, too. When the female spider lays her eggs, she winds silk around the eggs to keep them safe. The egg sack is stored in a place where it won't be hurt.

As the newborn spiders, or spiderlings, break free from their silk egg sacks, they trail silk threads behind them. Being a young spider is not easy. Hundreds of spiderlings may be born at one time, all clustered together, in the same area. The greatest threat comes from their own brothers and sisters, because the spiderlings are hungry. With no food around, they begin to eat each other.

The spiderlings scamper as fast as they can to the highest point they can find. Now they must wait for the wind. When the wind passes, it catches the silky threads that trail from their bodies, lifting the spiderlings into the air. This is called ballooning. The wind transports the young spiders to new places, where they will start to spin webs of their own.

A spiderling is

A a baby spider

C a female spider

B an egg sack

D a newborn spider

Look for a synonym for spiderling in the selection. The word *or* is a clue that spiderling is a synonym for *newborn spider*, choice D.

The word clustered means

A born

C living

B bunched

D cluttered

The sentence already tells you that the spiderlings are born together in one place. But the phrase *in the same area* gives you a clue that clustered means "bunched," choice B. Since there are hundreds of them, they must be very close together!

The word threat means

A problem

C hunger

B danger

D frighten

When you read the paragraph, you can find an example that tells you what threat means. The example is that the spiderlings eat each other. That's certainly a danger. Choice B is the correct answer.

Ballooning means

A lifting into the air

C spinning a web

B jumping off the ground

D crawling out of the sack

Look back at the sentence just before the one with the word ballooning. It is a definition of ballooning. Choice A is the correct answer.

Idioms

An **idiom** is a phrase that has a meaning different from the meaning of the words in the phrase. Read this sentence.

Rocco had to run to catch up with his class.

The actual meaning of the word catch is to receive something in your hands that another person has thrown. That meaning doesn't fit here. In this sentence, the phrase catch up is an idiom that means "move fast enough to reach other people."

Here are some other idioms you might know.

To be all ears		listen carefully.
To hang out with	**MEANS THE SAME AS**	be with.
To keep an eye on		to watch.
To take it easy		go slower.

You know and use many idioms. There are four idioms in the story below. Try to match each idiom with its meaning below the paragraph.

"Step on it!" Dad said, and we all raced to the car. "It will break Cara's heart if we're late for the pageant." All five of us kids got in our usual seats. Nobody wanted to miss the show. Dad started the car, and we hit the road.

We all began to talk at once. Dad said, "Now keep it down. I can't concentrate with all of you making noise."

started to go   hurry up   be quiet   hurt someone's feelings

Guided Practice

Read the following message and answer the questions that follow.

```
┌─────────────────────────────────────────────────────────────────────┐
│                    Alonzo's birthday – Message                    □ ▤ │
├─────────────────────────────────────────────────────────────────────┤
│  📧 Send   💾 Save    📇 ⬇ ᴬᴮᶜ    📎 Insert File...  ⬆ Priority ▾  ▤ Options... │
├─────────────────────────────────────────────────────────────────────┤
│  ℹ This mail message has not yet been sent.                        ✉ │
├─────────────────────────────────────────────────────────────────────┤
│  ┌─────────┐  ┌──────────────────────────────────────────────────┐  │
│  │  To...  │  │ Friends and Family   ⁻                           │  │
│  └─────────┘  └──────────────────────────────────────────────────┘  │
│  ┌─────────┐  ┌──────────────────────────────────────────────────┐  │
│  │  Cc...  │  │                                                  │  │
│  └─────────┘  └──────────────────────────────────────────────────┘  │
│  Subject:  ┌──────────────────────────────────────────────────────┐ │
│            │ Alonzo's birthday                                    │ │
│            └──────────────────────────────────────────────────────┘ │
├─────────────────────────────────────────────────────────────────────┤
│  Charcoal            ▲▼  12  ▲▼   B  I  U  ⊞▾  ⁞☰ ⬸ ⬷ │ ☰ ☰ ☰       │
├─────────────────────────────────────────────────────────────────────┤
```

Hi everyone,

    Saturday, June 4, is Alonzo's birthday. We are planning a surprise party for him at two o'clock. All his friends will <u>hang around</u> in his backyard. When Alonzo gets home from practice, his mom will <u>make believe</u> she needs something from the yard. And when Alonzo comes out, we'll all yell surprise!

    Please let me know if you can come. And if you see Alonzo before that, don't <u>let the cat out of the bag</u>!

Risa

The phrase <u>hang around</u> means to

A play games

B move around

C stay in one place

D hang decorations

> Everyone will be waiting for Alonzo to arrive. That tells you that to *hang around* means "to stay in one place," choice C. All of the other choices are too specific to fit in the context.

The phrase <u>make believe</u> means

A read aloud

C explain

B tell a lie

D pretend

You probably know this idiom because you used to "make believe" you were someone else when you were a child. So you can figure out that to <u>make believe</u> means "to pretend," choice D.

The phrase <u>let the cat out of the bag</u> means to

A give away a secret

C send an e-mail message

B let a cat out of a bag

D keep something to yourself

The context tells you that Risa wants to keep the surprise party a secret from Alonzo. So choice A is the correct answer.

Test Yourself

Read the following selection and answer the questions that follow.

The opossum is an unusual animal. Female opossums have a <u>pouch</u> like a kangaroo. This pocket is home to baby opossums for the first three months of their lives. After that they often <u>cling</u> to their mother's back for a free ride. There may be as many as 12 babies in a <u>litter</u> of opossums.

Opossums are interesting in other ways, too. On their back feet, they have a toe that is like our thumb. This toe, plus a long, strong tail, makes the opossum a good climber. Young opossums can even hang by their tails. Perhaps the most interesting thing about opossums is the way they "<u>play possum</u>." If a larger animal catches an opossum, the opossum will go limp. Its enemy thinks it's dead and drops the opossum. When it is safe, the opossum will "wake up" and <u>scurry</u> away.

Most people think opossums are <u>pests</u>. At night they turn over garbage cans, looking for food. They also crawl under porches and decks. Sometimes they are hard to get out. But opossums <u>thrive</u> by living near people. That's why you see so many of them!

Unit 1 Vocabulary Strategies

1 A <u>pouch</u> is similar to a

   A bag

   B pocket

   C mother

   D kangaroo

2 In which sentence does the word <u>litter</u> mean the same thing that it means in the article?

   A We are going to pick up the litter around the yard.

   B It is against the law to litter.

   C Our dog had a litter of six puppies.

   D The men put the big dog on a litter to take it to the vet.

3 What does the word <u>cling</u> mean?

   A hold on

   B jump on

   C ride on

   D climb on

4 The word <u>pests</u> tells you that people

   A are afraid of opossums

   B like to feed baby opossums

   C don't want to have opossums around their houses

   D believe that opossums are good for the environment

5 What does the phrase <u>play possum</u> mean?

   A to crawl under a deck

   B to play with an opossum

   C to imitate an opossum

   D to pretend to be dead

6 The word <u>scurry</u> means

   A to run fast

   B to wake up

   C to dig a hole

   D to turn around

7 To <u>thrive</u> means to

   A eat often

   B be successful

   C live near people

   D have many babies

Unit 1 Vocabulary Strategies

Unit 2: Reading and Writing for Information

Most of the reading you do is for information. Lessons 3–8 guide you through six important skills that will help you read and understand information. Lessons 9–12 help you learn to write well. You can use the skills from these lessons to help you answer test questions and in all the reading and writing you do.

3 Organizational Features Most books are organized with an index, table of contents, chapters, and paragraphs to help you find information you need. Organizational features such as boxes, heads, underlines, different fonts, and italic type help you sort out the text in short selections.

4 Finding the Sequence It's not always easy to figure out the sequence or order that things happen in a reading selection. Clue words and hints can help you.

5 Prior Knowledge Prior means "before." So prior knowledge means the things you already know before you begin to read. You can use your own knowledge and experience to help you understand what you read.

6 Main Idea and Details When you read, ask yourself, "What's the main point? What is this all about?" When you find the main idea, all the details come together.

7 Cause and Effect If you don't do your homework [cause], your grades will go down [effect]. To understand an article you will often need to look back for causes or figure them out. This lesson will show you how to find causes and effects.

8 Compare and Contrast When you compare and contrast things or ideas, you figure out how they are alike or different. You will learn to use graphic organizers to compare and contrast the information that you read.

9 The Writing Process This lesson guides you through the five steps of the writing process. You can use this process in all of your writing.

10 Editing a Paragraph It's important to go back over your writing to correct the mistakes. This lesson shows you how.

11 Writing a Short Response Sometimes you have to write a few sentences or a paragraph to answer a test question. Learn how to make every word count when you write a short answer.

12 Writing an Extended Response To answer some questions, you have to write a whole story or an essay. This lesson will guide you through writing long or extended responses.

Organizational Features

Standard 1.R.2, 4, 6, 11, 13

A book is divided into chapters. A chapter is divided into paragraphs. A table of contents helps you find the chapters. In a nonfiction book, you may want to find a specific word or name. That's what an index is for. These **organizational features** can help you to better understand what you are reading.

Even a short selection may have special features that organize information.

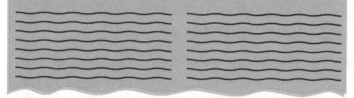

Headings in large bold type tell you about what follows.

Special information can be set off in a box or border.

A different style of type can also grab your attention.

- milk
- apples
- cookies
- oatmeal

Numbers or special symbols point out items on a list.

A picture or chart can help you understand what you're reading.

Guided Practice

See how organizational features help you understand this article. Then answer the questions that follow.

On the Go at the Seabrook Go Center

Serena Baerga places a stone while Colin Ohman waits his turn. Monday 6:00 to 9:00 p.m. is Children's Night at the Seabrook Go Center. Kids can have a friendly game or learn from experts.

A very old board game has a new home in our community. It's the Seabrook Go Center, which opened last month at Seabrook Mall.

Go is a game of strategy and skill. Two players take turns placing black or white stones on a wooden board. They try to capture territory. The winner is the player whose stones control the most territory.

A Hard Game with Easy Rules

"I learned about Go in a Japanese comic book," says Serena Baerga, age 10. "Now it's my favorite game. It's great to have a Go center at the mall. My school has a chess club, but nobody there plays Go."

That may change soon, thanks to the Center. Go is said to be more complicated than chess. But you can learn the rules in five minutes. Players are ranked according to skill. Stronger players may be given a handicap of up to 23 stones. That way, a beginner can have a chance against an expert.

Seabrook Go Center Facts, Figures

Where: Seabrook Mall

When: Monday–Friday 3:00–9:00 p.m., Saturday noon–10:00 p.m.

Fees: First three sessions free, then $5.00 for adults, $2.00 children under 18. Monthly and yearly rates available.

Lessons: By appointment

Contact information: (516) 555-4646 or www.goseabrook.org

A Game in History and Legend

Go began in China at least 3,000 years ago. The game is most popular in Japan. Records of games and top players have been kept there since the 1200s. The game figures in Japanese history and legend.

"Kings and queens used to play," Serena Baerga says. "There was even a Go Officer appointed by the ruler. His job was to rank players and arrange matches."

There are no kings or queens 'at the Seabrook Go Center. Everyone is welcome to play, watch, or learn. Expert players are on hand to teach the game or accept challenges.

This article tells us what the "stones" in Go are like by using

A   a picture of people playing the game

B   a chart showing the game's equipment

C   a description in the article

D   a diagram of a game

"One picture is worth a thousand words." The picture on page 27 shows that Go "stones" are small round counters. Otherwise you might think the article was talking about some kind of rocks. The correct answer is A.

To learn about the history of Go, you would look in this article for

A   a numbered list

B   an item in an index

C   information in a box

D   a paragraph under a heading

This article is too short to have an index. But it does have headings in bold type to help organize information. One of these easy-to-notice headings contains the word "history." So you can guess you'll find what you want under that heading. Choice D is the correct answer.

Unit 2 Reading and Writing for Information

The article tells us about Children's Night at the Go center by using

A   information in a box

B   questions and answers

C   the caption of the picture

D   a paragraph with the heading "Children"

> The box at the right does contain some information about children at the Go center. But the information you're looking for is in the caption of the picture. It tells us that Children's Night is Monday from 6:00 to 9:00 p.m. Choice C is the correct answer.

What does the information in the box tell you about the Go center?

_____

_____

_____

_____

_____

_____

On a separate sheet of paper, write an article or advertisement about your favorite game. Use at least three organizational features.

Test Yourself

Now read an article about snow and answer the questions that follow.

Chris McDonald knows snow. He enjoys snowmobiling and skiing. He's also a weather scientist. So when he wants the most of the white stuff, he knows just where to go. In this interview, he talks about the Tug Hill Plateau and why it gets so much snow.

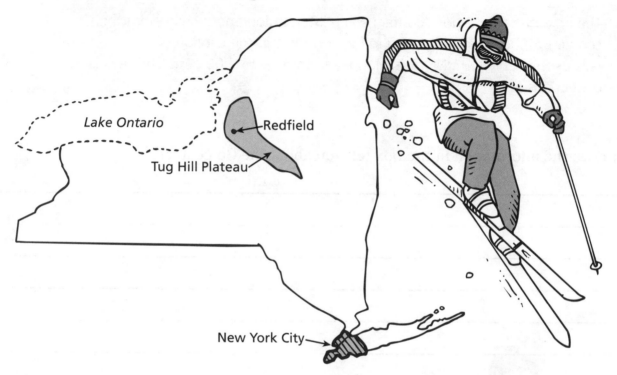

Interviewer: Is the Tug Hill Plateau the snowiest place in America?

Chris: No. There are places in the Rocky Mountains and in the Northwest that get more snow. But it's probably the snowiest place in the eastern states. It's certainly the snowiest in New York State.

Interviewer: Why is that?

Chris: It's called the lake effect. You've got Lake Ontario to the west. It's so big that it doesn't freeze over. So you've got moisture rising from it all winter long. Then you've got the Tug Hill Plateau itself. It's 2,100 feet high. When the wind blows from the west, it picks up moisture from the lake. When it gets to Tug Hill, the moisture freezes, and you get a lot of snow.

Interviewer: How much snow is "a lot"?

Chris: I think the one-day record is more than six feet. A few years ago when I was snowmobiling up near Redfield, there was snow up to the telephone wires.

Interviewer: That's a lot! How do people who live there deal with it?

Chris: Well, they don't shovel it off their sidewalks every morning. Actually, not many people live on the Tug Hill Plateau. It's pretty rural. A lot of it is covered by forest. None of the towns have more than a few hundred people. They lock their cars in the garage all winter and get around by snowmobile. And a lot of businesses rent snow equipment to people like me who come up from the city. Every town has its snowmobile club.

Interviewer: How did you get to like snow so much?

Chris: Doesn't everyone?

> ### Tug Hill Snow Records
> ❄ **winter:** 467 inches at Hooker, 1976–77
> ❄ **month:** 192 inches at Bennett Bridges, January 1978
> ❄ **storm:** 95 inches at Montague, January 10–14, 1997
> ❄ **day:** 77 inches at Montague, January 12, 1997

1 This article tells you why Tug Hill Plateau gets so much snow by using

   A a map

   B a graph

   C pictures and charts

   D questions and answers

2 The paragraph in *italic type* at the beginning of the article tells you

   A who Chris McDonald is

   B where the Tug Hill Plateau is

   C where you can rent snowmobiles

   D how you can get to the Tug Hill Plateau

3 Which of these does the information in the box tell you?

   A how much snow fell at Montague last winter

   B how much the average snowfall is at Tug Hill

   C the biggest snowfall ever in New York State

   D the most snow ever recorded at Tug Hill in one day

4 The information in the box is made easier to understand because it uses

    A a large headline

    B a list with numbers

    C a list with special symbols

    D a chart showing snowfall in inches

5 How does the map help you understand Chris McDonald's explanation of why the Tug Hill Plateau gets so much snow?

_____

_____

_____

_____

_____

_____

6 On a separate sheet of paper, write a paragraph describing what you like to do best on a snowy day.

Unit 2 Reading and Writing for Information

Finding the Sequence

Standard 1.R.3, 12; 1.W.3

In your life things happen in order.

You get up. → You eat breakfast. → You get dressed. → You go to school.

The order in which things happen is called **sequence.** When you read, you need to follow the sequence of events or steps. Whether you are reading about someone's life, the steps of a science experiment, or a story, you need to be able to follow the sequence.

Events in reading selections are not always written in order. An author may begin by telling you something that happened recently and then go back to earlier events. Watch for dates, time words, and other clues that can help you place events or steps in order. Writing events or steps on a timeline like the one above can also help you find the sequence.

Look for *sequence* words	
first	recently
second	earlier
third	later
last	finally
next	now
before	after
following	then

Guided Practice

Read a biography. Then answer the questions that follow.

Shirley Chisholm died on New Year's Day 2005. Hundreds of people attended her funeral in New York City. Some remembered her as "Fighting Shirley Chisholm." That was her slogan when she won her first election for Congress in 1968. Some remembered her as the first African American to run for president. That happened in 1972. And some remembered her as their preschool teacher in the 1950s.

She was born Shirley St. Hill in Brooklyn in 1924. As a child, she lived with her grandmother on the West Indian island of Barbados. Later she returned to New York to attend high school and college. In 1949 she married Conrad Chisholm.

Chisholm was a day care worker until 1959. Then she became active in politics. She started the Democratic Unity Club. The club organized people to vote.

Unit 2 Reading and Writing for Information

Then in 1964, she ran for political office herself. She was elected to the New York State Assembly. After two terms, she ran for the U.S. Congress. She became the first African American woman ever elected to Congress. She served 14 years. She proudly called herself "unbossed and unbought." She meant that she owed no favors to anyone in power. She worked hard for equal rights for all Americans. *Unbossed and Unbought* was also the title of her first book. It was published in 1970.

Chisholm left Congress in 1982. Afterward, she worked as a college teacher. She was also in demand as a speaker and a political advisor. She lived her last years in Florida.

Among the people at her funeral were African American members of Congress from across America. "Perhaps if there was not a Shirley Chisholm, I would not be a member of the United States Congress," Representative Julia Carson of Indiana said.

Which of these did Shirley Chisholm do first?

A She ran for president.

B She worked as a college teacher.

C She worked as a preschool teacher.

D She won her first election for Congress.

In this biography, dates given in years are clues that tell you the sequence of Shirley Chisholm's life. So are words like *later, then,* and *last.* Chisholm worked as a preschool teacher in the 1950s. That was earlier than the dates of the other choices. So choice C is the correct answer.

Shirley Chisholm wrote her book *Unbossed and Unbought*

A after she lived in Florida

B before she ran for president

C after she left the U.S. Congress

D before her first race for Congress

Here again, you can use the dates and clue words to find the sequence. Chisholm published *Unbossed and Unbought* in 1970. Find the clues that tell you when each of the other events happened. The only answer that works is "before she ran for president." Choice B is the correct answer.

Which of the following should fill the empty box in the timeline?

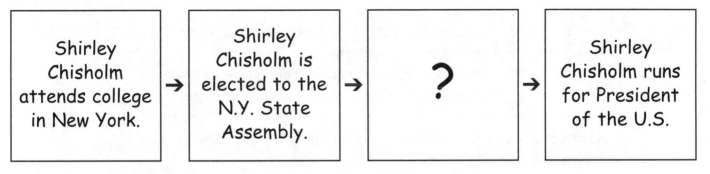

| Shirley Chisholm attends college in New York. | → | Shirley Chisholm is elected to the N.Y. State Assembly. | → | ? | → | Shirley Chisholm runs for President of the U.S. |

A   Shirley marries Conrad Chisholm.

B   Shirley Chisholm is elected to Congress.

C   Shirley Chisholm lives in Barbados.

D   Shirley Chisholm starts the Democratic Unity Club.

> You often find timeline questions like this on reading tests. They are like any other sequencing questions. Use the dates, time words, and other clues to find which of the four choices falls correctly in the sequence. Here the correct answer is choice B.

Which words or phrases tell you when Shirley Chisholm lived in Barbados? Explain your answer.

_____

_____

_____

_____

_____

_____

Use a separate sheet of paper. Write a short biography of a member of your family. Include at least six events. Use dates and other time words that show the sequence.

Now find the sequence in these directions and answer the questions that follow.

The fourth-grade picnic will be Saturday at MacAdam State Park from noon until dark. To get there from school, take Fifth Street north to the Loness Expressway. Follow the expressway west to the Marshall Road exit. Turn left at the stop sign. Follow Marshall Road about two miles to County Road 523. Turn right. After about one-half mile, you'll see the park entrance on your left. Follow the signs to the picnic area.

To get to the picnic area from school, which do you do second?

A Go west on the Loness Expressway.

B Take the Marshall Road exit.

C Turn left at the stop sign.

D Take Fifth Street north.

Read the directions carefully. The first thing you do is to take Fifth Street north to the Loness Expressway. The second thing you do is to follow the expressway west. So choice A is the correct answer.

You turn right onto County Road 523

A after you see the park entrance

B before you turn left at the stop sign

C before you get on the Loness Expressway

D after driving two miles on Marshall Road

If you read the directions carefully, you'll see that you turn onto County Road 523 from Marshall Road after you've gone about two miles. Choice D is the correct answer.

What do you do after you see the state park entrance?

_____

_____

_____

Use a separate sheet of paper. Write a set of directions for getting someplace from your school. Include a sequence of at least five steps.

Unit 2 Reading and Writing for Information

Test Yourself

Read these instructions about how to do a magic trick. Answer the questions that follow.

The Dream Card
by Shelby Reason

"The Dream Card" is an old magician's trick. In fact, it's so old your friends probably have never seen it!

Give your friend a deck of cards. Ask her to shuffle them. Then tell her, "I had this funny dream last night. I dreamed about a card. I want to find the card I dreamed about. Please hold up the deck so that the cards are facing me. Then pass them one at a time to your other hand so I can see each face. Stop when I tell you."

The first two cards your friend shows you are the key to the trick. The first card will be the *number* of your dream card. The second will be the *suit* of your dream card. In the picture, the first card is the *queen* of diamonds. The second is the five of *clubs*. So your dream card is the *queen of clubs*. (If the first two cards turn out to be of the same suit, tell your friend to shuffle the deck and start again.)

Have your friend keep passing the cards one by one to the other hand with the faces showing. When your dream card appears, say, "Stop!" Take the card without letting your friend see it. Place it face down on the table between you. Then take the cards from her hands and place them together face down on the table. *Make sure that the part of the deck she has already passed is on top.* The first two cards she showed you will now be on top of the deck.

Next, you say, "I'll bet you can guess which card I dreamed about. Start dealing the cards one at a time face down. Stop whenever you feel like it." Your friend starts dealing them into a pile on the table. Your two key cards are now on the bottom of the pile.

Now tell your friend, "Pick up the cards you have dealt. Deal them evenly, one at a time, into two piles." Your two key cards will end up on the top of the two piles. Note carefully where the last card goes. Point to that pile and say, "The top card in this pile will show the *number* of my dream card." Your friend turns it up—it's a queen. Then point to the other pile and say, "The top card in this pile will show the *suit* of my dream card." Your friend turns it up—it's a club.

Now you turn up your dream card. "Exactly right!" you tell your astonished friend. "It's the queen of clubs! You can read my dreams!"

1 Which of these do you do first?

A Note the first two cards your friend shows you.

B Figure out what your "dream card" will be.

C Tell your friend about your "dream."

D Have your friend shuffle the deck.

2 You tell your friend to "Stop!"

A before you know what the dream card will be

B after your friend shows you the dream card

C after you take the cards from your friend

D after your friend deals out two piles

3 Which of these is the last thing you say?

A "The top card in this pile will show the *suit* of my dream card."

B "Deal them evenly, one at a time, into two piles."

C "Please hold up the deck so that the cards are facing me."

D "I'll bet you can guess which card I dreamed about."

Use this story map to do Number 4.

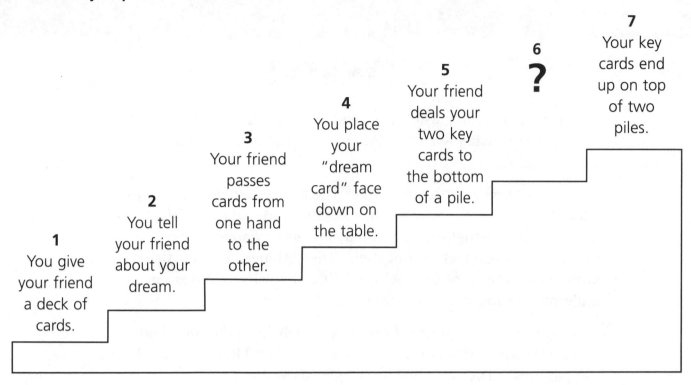

1 You give your friend a deck of cards.

2 You tell your friend about your dream.

3 Your friend passes cards from one hand to the other.

4 You place your "dream card" face down on the table.

5 Your friend deals your two key cards to the bottom of a pile.

6 ?

7 Your key cards end up on top of two piles.

4 Which of these best fits as Step 6?

   A You say, "Stop!"

   B Your friend shuffles the cards.

   C Your friend deals the cards into two piles.

   D Your friend turns up the top card in each pile.

5 What is an important instruction in the trick that is not part of the sequence? Explain why it is important.

_____

_____

_____

_____

6 Use a separate sheet of paper. Make up directions that tell a friend how to do something. Use time words as clues to the sequence of steps. Be sure to include at least seven steps.

Your mind is busy when you read. You may not be aware of it, but you're always using what you know to help you understand what you're reading.

Suppose you start reading an article about planets. You may know a lot about planets. You may have seen pictures of them. Maybe you have visited a planetarium. You may know the names of several planets and a few facts about them. These things are your **prior knowledge.** (*Prior* means "before.") Prior knowledge helps you understand what you're reading.

As you read, ask yourself questions such as: "What do I know about this subject? What do I think about when I look at the title and the pictures?" Then use this knowledge as you read.

Guided Practice

Read this selection. Use what you know to answer the questions that follow.

The cheetah is the fastest land animal. But if a cheetah raced another animal, which animal would come in second? That would be the pronghorn.

The pronghorn is a grass-eating mammal, related to the antelope. It gets its name from the males' long, upward-pointing horns. It lives on the plains of the American west. It is reddish brown with a dark mane and white bands and patches.

The pronghorn is *fast.* It has been clocked at nearly 54 miles per hour (87 km per hour). But its speed could not protect it from hunters. By the 1920s, the pronghorn was an endangered species. Then laws were passed to protect it. Today, nearly a million pronghorn live wild in Wyoming, Nebraska, and other western states.

The article says that the cheetah is the fastest land animal. A cheetah is like a big

A deer

C rabbit

B horse

D cat

> The article assumes that you know what a cheetah is. And you probably do. It's a large member of the cat family that hunts on the plains of Africa. The correct answer is choice D.

A pronghorn can run at a speed of nearly 54 miles per hour. This is about as fast as a

A human runner

C car

B bicycle

D airplane

> The figure "54 miles per hour" lets you picture how fast a pronghorn runs. You know that a car on the highway may go about that speed. Choice C is the correct answer.

The pronghorn lives in Wyoming and Nebraska. If you didn't know where these places are, you could find out by looking at

A a dictionary

C a wildlife encyclopedia

B a United States map

D an article about endangered species

> You may already know where Wyoming and Nebraska are. But in case you don't, the article tells you that they're "on the plains of the American west." You could find these states on a United States map. The correct answer is B.

The article tells you that the pronghorn is a mammal. What are some other animals that are mammals? What makes an animal a mammal?

_____

_____

_____

_____

Now use what you know to answer the questions that follow this selection.

It's a Party!

Come help celebrate Jonas's 10th birthday. Join us on Saturday, May 21, from 3:00 to 6:00 p.m. The party will be at Game Circus, 600 Fourth Avenue. There will be pizza, cake, ice cream, and two hours of mini-golf and video games. RSVP to Jonas's mom, 518-555-7832 or rosemariey@bpm.com by Thursday, May 19. (Please DO NOT call Game Circus!) Hope you can join in our fun.

This selection is **best** described as

A   an invitation

B   a thank-you note

C   a friendly letter

D   an advertisement

That's an easy one. You've probably been going to birthday parties ever since you can remember. A thank-you note is what Jonas would send someone *after* his party. This is an invitation asking someone to come to his party. Choice A is correct.

To contact Jonas's mom at rosemariey@bpm.com, you would need a

A   stamp

B   telephone

C   computer

D   name and address

You probably also know what an e-mail address is. You know that to send an e-mail, you need a computer. The correct answer is choice C. Using what you know could help make sure there's a place for you at the party.

Game Circus is at 600 Fourth Avenue. If you didn't know where that was, you could find out by looking at

A a street map

B a United States map

C a telephone book

D a newspaper

To find where a place is, you need a map. You'd use a U.S. map to find a state. But 600 Fourth Avenue is a street address. To find it you'd need a map of the town or city that shows where the different streets are. Choice A is the correct answer.

The invitation says to "RSVP to Jonas's mom." What does this instruction mean?

_____

_____

_____

_____

_____

_____

_____

What would be the perfect birthday party for you? On a separate sheet of paper, write a paragraph describing it.

Test Yourself

Now read another selection. Use what you know to answer the questions that follow.

April 10

    Well, I can finally believe we're in New York City! We arrived yesterday. Aunt Stefani met us at the airport. We went straight to their house in Brooklyn. (It's great to see her and Uncle Lester and Celia again.) Then as soon as we had some lunch, we started touring! They live not far from the New York Aquarium, so that's where we went first. It was fun, but I've been to aquariums before. And I know Brooklyn is part of New York City. But nothing I saw looked like the New York I know from TV and movies.

    Today was different! Uncle Lester announced that we were going to Manhattan for the day. That's the "New York" part of New York. First we took the subway. When we got out, we were still in Brooklyn. But we could see the tall buildings of New York across a river. Way off in the distance to the left was the Statue of Liberty. (We're supposed to go there later this week.) Then we started to walk. We walked across the Brooklyn Bridge into Manhattan. Soon we were in the middle of all the tall buildings.

    Uncle L. wanted us to see the old African Burial Ground. Well, I thought, I didn't come all the way to New York to see a cemetery! But it turned out to be a special place after all. It's really a museum where the cemetery used to be. (Most of the graves are still underneath the tall buildings.) The land was a burying place for African Americans in the 1700s. Uncle L. is proud that some of our family was living in New York way back then.

    We had lunch at another old place that's *not* under the ground. It's called Fraunces Tavern. It's both a museum and a restaurant. George Washington ate there. And so did I! I had a really great cheeseburger. I bet they didn't have cheeseburgers in the 1700s.

We walked all afternoon. We saw parks and the Stock Exchange and Greenwich Village. Maybe it was a real village when the African Burial Ground was really a burial ground. Today it's a crowded neighborhood. Finally we took the subway back to Brooklyn.

There's lots more to see here. Aunt S. tells me we'll see it all. She wants to show us the art museums and Central Park. Celia is eager to show me Coney Island. Right now, I'm happy to rest my feet!

1 This selection is in the form of

A a Web page

B a friendly letter

C a diary entry

D a magazine article

2 The selection mentions the New York Aquarium. Which of these would you expect to see at an aquarium?

A dinosaur skeletons

B fish and penguins

C great works of art

D a show with dancing

3 If you didn't know what an aquarium was and wanted to find out, you could look in

A a dictionary

B a book on history

C a map of New York City

D a wildlife encyclopedia

4 The author writes about two places that date from the 1700s. What are some facts that you know about life in America at that time?

_____

_____

_____

_____

_____

_____

_____

5 On a separate sheet of paper, write a paragraph about a place that you would like to visit. Tell why you want to go there and what you'd expect to see.

 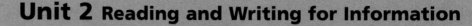

Main Idea and Details

Everything you read is *about* something. Think of the last book you read. You can probably tell what it was about in one or two sentences—even if it was a long book. It's the same with each chapter in the book. It's even the same with individual paragraphs. Each one has a **main idea,** the idea that the passage is about.

In many paragraphs, there is one sentence that expresses the most important idea. It is called the **topic sentence.** It is usually the first or last sentence of the paragraph. But it could be any sentence or none at all. The other sentences in a paragraph are details that support or explain the topic sentence. Some paragraphs do not have a topic sentence, only details.

- Main idea questions usually ask you to choose the best summary of the main idea. A summary will state the main idea in a different way. Look for the answer that tells what the entire selection or paragraph is about, not just the details.

- Some main idea questions ask you to choose a title for the selection or for part of the selection.

Guided Practice

Read this article. Then answer the questions that follow.

The octopus may be the smartest of all the invertebrates. These are the animals without backbones. Everyone knows that an octopus has eight arms and two large eyes. But it also has a well-developed brain.

Many fish prey on the soft-bodied octopus. But the octopus has ways of protecting itself. It hides in holes and under rocks. It can change the color of its skin quickly. When attacked, it squirts out a cloud of black ink.

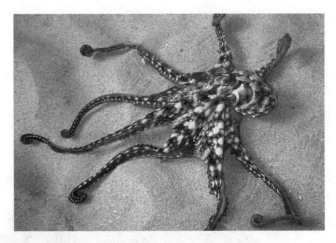

An octopus comes out of hiding only to eat or mate. It eats sea animals such as clams and shrimp. It may sneak up on its prey and pounce on it. Or, it may wiggle the tip of one arm like a worm to attract its food.

Which sentence tells the main idea of the first paragraph?

A The octopus may be the smartest of all the invertebrates.

B These are the animals without backbones.

C Everyone knows that an octopus has eight arms and two large eyes.

D But it also has a well-developed brain.

In this paragraph, the first sentence is the topic sentence. It expresses the main idea of the paragraph. The other sentences either explain or support the first sentence. Choice B explains what "invertebrates" means. Choices C and D give more information about octopuses. So choice A is the correct answer.

In the second paragraph, which sentence tells the main idea?

A Many fish prey on the soft-bodied octopus.

B But the octopus has ways of protecting itself.

C It hides in holes and under rocks.

D When attacked, it squirts out a cloud of black ink.

This time the topic sentence is the second sentence of the paragraph. The other sentences all support the topic sentence. Choice A tells why the octopus needs to protect itself. Choices C and D describe ways it protects itself. The correct answer is choice B.

The third paragraph is **mostly** about

A why an octopus comes out of hiding

B what an octopus eats

C how an octopus finds food

D where an octopus lives

The third paragraph has no topic sentence. It mostly describes ways that the octopus hunts. Supporting sentences explain what it hunts and state that feeding is one of the only reasons it comes out of hiding. Choice C correctly describes the main idea of the paragraph.

Sometimes it helps to be able to **paraphrase** the main idea of a selection in your own words. When you explain all the important events and details, you're **summarizing** the selection.

How would you summarize part of a book when describing it in a book report? How would you choose what was most important?

On his way, Niles has many adventures.

Which of these details is **most** important to include in a summary of the article on page 47 about octopuses?

A   Invertebrates are animals without backbones.

B   An octopus has eight arms and two large eyes.

C   The octopus has a well-developed brain.

D   The octopus is preyed on by many fish.

The article is mostly about the octopus's intelligence. Choices A, B, and D are facts that do not support the main idea. Choice C helps explain the main idea. That's why it's important to include it in a summary. Choice C is the correct answer.

Write a title for the article on page 47. Explain why it is a good title.

_____

_____

_____

_____

_____

_____

_____

Now read a notice and answer the questions that follow.

Reserve Your Garden Plot!

Neighborhood Meeting at Banneker Elementary School

Attention flower and vegetable lovers! The city has agreed to set aside the vacant lot at 23rd and Florence for a community garden. Reserve your 10- by 15-foot garden plot at a meeting at 7:30 Thursday evening March 4 at Banneker Elementary School, 2100 Stearns Ave.

Who Is Eligible?

Any family living in the Brugen neighborhood qualifies for a plot. (See map.) Bring proof of address, such as a phone bill. There are 20 plots available. A drawing for the plots will be held at the meeting. Anyone who does not win a plot will be put on a waiting list.

Rules and Tools

Winners must use and keep up their plots. Otherwise, plots may be assigned to someone on the waiting list. The Brugen Neighborhood Club will provide soil, wheelbarrows, and hoses. You must supply your own gardening tools. Sorry, no poisonous chemicals allowed.

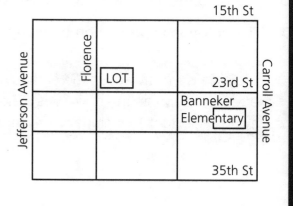

Brugen Neighborhood Club   (718) 555-7295   brugenneighbors@bxm.org

Which of these details from the first paragraph does **not** belong in a summary of the notice?

A   A meeting will be held at Banneker Elementary School.

B   You can reserve a plot in a community garden.

C   The plots are 10 feet by 15 feet in size.

D   The meeting is at 7:30 in the evening of March 4.

> The main idea is what the meeting is for. The supporting facts are where and when it will take place. You don't have to know the size of the garden plot to come to the meeting. So the correct answer is C.

Which of these details is important to include in a summary?

A   You have to show that you live in the Brugen neighborhood.

B   Those who don't win the drawing will be put on a waiting list.

C   The Brugen Neighborhood Club will provide some tools.

D   No poisonous chemicals are allowed.

> The "rules and tools" information is useful for people who win the drawing. But it's most important to note that the garden is only for people who live in the Brugen neighborhood. If someone can't prove that she lives in the neighborhood, she will waste her time coming to the meeting. Choice A is the correct answer.

Write a summary of the notice in your own words. Be sure to include important facts and details about the notice.

_____

_____

_____

_____

_____

On a separate sheet of paper, write your own notice about a meeting (real or imaginary). Be sure to include all important facts and details.

Test Yourself

Now read an article and answer the questions that follow.

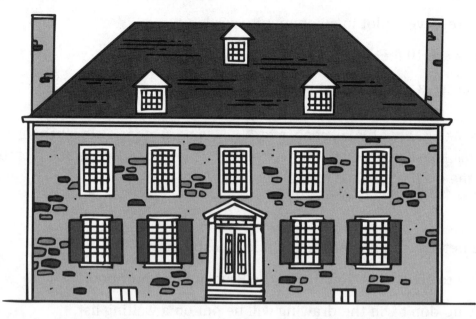

At Fort Johnson, you'll visit a house that's over 250 years old. You'll see rooms furnished as they were when it was new. You'll see tools, weapons, and crafts of early America. George Washington visited this house once. He may even have used the privy, or outdoor restroom, which still stands. At least, people around here say he did.

Fort Johnson stands near Amsterdam, New York. Nearby flows the Mohawk River. In colonial days, the river was a busy highway. That's why William Johnson built this house in 1742.

Johnson was an English soldier and trader. He owned a lot of land in the Mohawk Valley. He traded with Native Americans and settlers. Johnson wanted to preserve peace in the region. Because he learned their language and traded honestly, he won the trust of the powerful Iroquois people. He married an Iroquois woman in the Iroquois way. When he held regular meetings with Iroquois leaders at Fort Johnson, he wore Iroquois clothing. He helped make peace between the Iroquois and their enemies. When war broke out against France, he led Iroquois warriors in battle. The British government named him their official representative among all the Native American peoples. He became Sir William Johnson.

Sir William died in 1774. Soon afterward, America's War of Independence from England began. American patriots tore the lead roof off Fort Johnson to make bullets. The furniture was sold. But the sturdy old house remained.

In 1905, people began restoring it as a museum. They were able to buy back some of the Johnson family's original possessions. At Fort Johnson today, you'll see the house restored almost as it was when Sir William lived there. The original kitchen is still there. A table is set for supper. Colonial and Native American items from the region are on display. Guides dressed in costumes of the time show you the rooms.

One fascinating item at Fort Johnson dates from 1833. It's a faded work of art in a second-floor bedroom. A girl named Mary Ann Pierson made it. It's a sampler—a picture made by stitching colored yarn in cloth. There are animals, flowers, trees, an alphabet, and this rhyme by ten-year-old Mary:

Children look and see
What care my parents took of me,
That gave me learning in my youth
That I might learn to practice truth.

1 Which sentence tells the main idea of the first paragraph?

   A   At Fort Johnson, you'll visit a house that's over 250 years old.

   B   You'll see rooms furnished as they were when it was new.

   C   You'll see tools, weapons, and crafts of early America.

   D   George Washington visited this house once.

2 Which is the topic sentence of the second paragraph?

   A   Fort Johnson stands near Amsterdam, New York.

   B   Nearby flows the Mohawk River.

   C   In colonial days, the river was a busy highway.

   D   That's why William Johnson built this house in 1742.

3 The main idea of the third paragraph is that

   A   Johnson was an English trader and soldier

   B   Johnson won the respect of Native Americans

   C   Johnson built the biggest house in the area

   D   in Johnson's day, New York was ruled by England

4 What is this article mostly about? Explain your answer.

_____

_____

_____

_____

_____

5 Which paragraph does **not** contain any facts that need to be included in a summary of the article?

A paragraph 2   **C** paragraph 4

B paragraph 3   **D** paragraph 5

6 Which of these facts about the sampler in the last paragraph would be **most** important to include in a summary?

A It is not from Sir William Johnson's time.

B It was made by a ten-year-old girl.

C It is a picture made in yarn stitched on cloth.

D It is located in a second-floor bedroom.

7 Write a summary of the article. Include the main idea and a few important supporting details.

_____

_____

_____

_____

_____

8 Use a separate sheet of paper. Write a paragraph about a museum you have visited or would like to visit. Be sure to include details that support your topic sentence.

Cause and Effect

When you read, you probably see connections between ideas and events. These connections explain why things happen. Your reading makes more sense when you understand these *why* connections. Look for clue words that signal **cause and effect.** The thing that happens is the **effect.** The reason it happens, or what made it happen, is the **cause.**

Cause

Effect

These clue words signal causes:

because, since, reason for,

due to, on account of

These clue words signal effects:

then, so, led to, as a result,

in order that

Sometimes there are no clue words. Then you may need to draw a conclusion. Ask yourself "why did this event happen?" (That's the cause.) Then think, "what happened because of the event?" (That's the effect.) It might help to mentally add your own clue word ("because" or "so").

Guided Practice

Read this passage about a fish. Answer the questions that follow.

Wildlife experts are worried on account of a fish. The Asian carp is about to invade the Great Lakes. This fish is not native to America. So, it has no natural predators here. It was brought into the southern states about 10 years ago, in order to control disease and algae in the Mississippi River. It was kept in fish farms. But then the river flooded. As a result, some carp escaped. They multiplied and spread. They moved up the Mississippi and Illinois rivers. They average four feet in length and 60 pounds in weight. They eat almost anything. They crowd out the native fish. They even harm people who are fishing. When frightened by boats, they may jump 10 feet out of the water.

Now the Asian carp is 50 miles from the Great Lakes. It has been kept out only because of an electric fence. The fence lies across a canal near Chicago. It works because the fish sense it and swim away. The fence was an experiment. It was not built to last. It was expected to wear out in a few years. The U.S. government promised a permanent fence. But it has not provided money to build it. If Asian carp get into the lakes, they could eat their way through stocks of food fish. That's why wildlife experts call this fish "a disaster waiting to happen."

Look for *cause-and-effect* **words:**	
because	then
since	so
reason for	led to
due to	as a result
on account of	in order to

Why was the Asian carp brought to the United States?

A to be raised for food

B to be kept on farms

C to eat smaller fish

D to control disease

> The carp being brought to the United States is the cause. What is the effect? The first paragraph states that it happened in order to control disease and algae in the Mississippi River. Notice the words *in order to* in that sentence. That's a signal that the statement of the effect follows. So choice D is correct.

The carp escaped from fish farms because

    A a fence was damaged

    B the river flooded

    C they moved up the river

    D they eat almost anything

Here the word *because* tells you that you're looking for a cause. The passage tells you that some fish escaped *as a result* of something. The previous sentence tells you: *The river flooded.* Choice C is an effect of the fish escaping, not a cause. Choices A and D have nothing to do with the effect. So choice B is correct.

Since the carp are so big and eat almost anything,

    A they crowd out the native fish

    B they have no natural predators

    C they are easily frightened by boats

    D they would not survive in the Great Lakes

The word *since* tells you that you're looking for an effect. What is the effect of the fish being so big and eating almost everything? The passage does not tell you directly. But you can infer that the effect is what is stated in the next sentence: "They crowd out the native fish." Mentally test each choice with the word *so*. Choice A is the only answer that makes sense. It is the correct answer.

Why does the Asian carp have wildlife experts worried? Give details from the article to support your answer.

_____

_____

_____

_____

_____

_____

_____

Now read about a science experiment and answer the questions that follow.

Here's an experiment that can teach you something about forces. You can roll an empty can away from you and make it come back. You need a can with a replaceable lid, a rubber band, a hammer, and a nail.

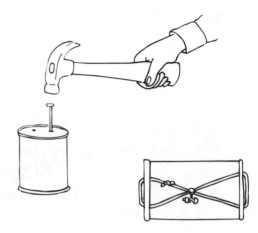

Start by hammering two holes in the lid with the nail. Then hammer two holes in the bottom. Remove the lid. Cut the rubber band to make one straight piece. (Or, tie together a few shorter ones.) Pass the two ends through the holes in the lid. Cross them inside the can to form a figure 8. Now pass them through the holes on the bottom. Tie the two ends together again. Now tie a piece of metal or other small weight to the place where the rubber bands cross. Replace the lid.

Roll the can away from you. Due to the weight, the can has a lower center of gravity. So it rolls with greater force. The rolling action and the weight cause the rubber band to wind up. There is a point at which the force of the rolling can exactly balances the force in the wound-up rubber band. At that point, the rubber band will start to unwind. So the can will roll back to you.

You can show the results to your friends as a magic trick. "I can make this can obey my commands!" you say. But it's really obeying the laws of forces. Try it with rubber bands of different sizes. The thicker the band, the faster the can will roll back.

Look for *cause-and-effect* **words:**	
because	then
since	so
reason for	led to
due to	as a result
on account of	in order to

What gives the can a lower center of gravity?

A the holes

B the rubber band

C the weight

D the rolling action

The lowered center of gravity is the effect. What is the cause? Look at paragraph three. The phrase *due to* is the clue. It tells you that the *weight* gives the can the lowered center of gravity. So choice C is the correct answer.

The rubber band unwinds inside the can. This is the reason that

A the can moves faster

C the forces are exactly balanced

B the can rolls back to you

D you want to use a long rubber band

> The phrase *the reason that* tells you that you're looking for an effect. "The rubber band unwinds" is the cause. Toward the end of the second paragraph, the word *so* signals the effect: "the can will roll back to you." Try *so* with the other answer choices. The last paragraph tells you what will make the can roll faster (choice A). Choices C and D do not make sense. Choice B is the correct answer.

You need a can with a replaceable lid because

A it's safer than using a can with a cut-off top

B it makes it easier to hammer the holes in

C you have to hang the weight where the rubber band crosses

D you have to remove the lid to set up the experiment

> Here, no clue words point directly to the cause. Think about why you need to have a lid that comes on and off. You need to take the lid off to run the rubber band through it. You need to have it on to do the experiment. Test all the answer choices in your mind. Choice D is the only one that makes sense. It is the correct answer.

What do you do to **cause** the can to roll with greater force? What is the **effect** of its rolling? Use details from the article in your answer.

_____

_____

_____

_____

_____

Use a separate sheet of paper. Write a paragraph explaining how something works. Include at least two statements of causes and effects.

Test Yourself

Now read an article about a historic fort. Answer the questions that follow.

Fort Ticonderoga

Fort Ticonderoga isn't easy to get to. It's on a narrow neck of land between Lake George and Lake Champlain. That's in upstate New York, about 250 miles north of New York City. No main highway passes near the place. Still, it draws more than 90,000 visitors each year. That's due to what happened there on May 10, 1775.

Fort Ticonderoga *was* on a main highway then. It was a highway of water. Native Americans, explorers, and traders traveled it in canoes. It was the easiest route between New York and Canada. But there were places along the way where there was no water. One of them was the narrow neck of land the Iroquois called Ticonderoga—"the place between two waters." Whoever controlled it controlled the route. Native Americans occupied the site thousands of years ago. The French built the fort there in 1755. A nearby waterfall sounded to their ears like a musical instrument called a carillon. So they named the place Fort Carillon. Four years later, during the French and Indian War, the British captured the fort. They named it Fort Ticonderoga.

Fort Ticonderoga is shaped like a star. Many forts of the 1700s were built that way. That was in order to let soldiers shoot at attackers from all directions. But many defenders were needed for that plan to work. On May 10, 1775, there were fewer than 50 men in the fort. And why should there be more than that? Britain was not at war. The French had been driven out of Canada in the last war. The Iroquois were friends. The fort was in Britain's own colony of New York. So few defenders were there. That morning, they were sleeping late. A gate had been left unlocked.

What the British didn't know was that they *were* at war. Fighting had broken out between British soldiers and American patriots. It had happened three weeks earlier near Boston. It was the beginning of America's War of Independence.

Ethan Allen got word before the British did. A patriot force had arrived from Connecticut. They had orders to capture the fort because of the weapons stored there. Allen was the leader of a group of patriots in nearby Vermont. They called themselves the Green Mountain Boys. They refused to fight under any leader but Allen. So he took charge.

Allen's Green Mountain Boys walked right into Fort Ticonderoga through the unlocked gate. The defenders were taken by surprise. One shot was fired—probably by accident. The fort was in American hands. The weapons were taken to Boston to be used in the fighting there.

Fort Ticonderoga is a museum today. In fact, it has been drawing visitors since the 1820s. Guides in costumes lead tours. There are exhibits of weapons and everyday objects from the 1700s. Some days you might even see a battle. It isn't a real battle, of course. It's a re-enactment, like a play, based on Fort Ticonderoga's history.

1 The location of Fort Ticonderoga was important in the 1700s because

   A several battles were fought there

   B it was the only nearby source of fresh water

   C it was only about 250 miles from New York City

   D it controlled the main route between New York and Canada

2 Because of what happened on May 10, 1775,

   A America's War of Independence began

   B the fort was named Fort Ticonderoga

   C many people visit Fort Ticonderoga

   D many soldiers lost their lives at the fort

3 Because a waterfall sounded like a musical instrument,

    A the French decided to build a fort nearby

    B the fort was the location for a lot of parties

    C the French named the place Fort Carillon

    D the British captured the fort from the French

Use this graphic organizer to answer Question 4.

What happened	Why it happened
Fort Ticonderoga was built in the shape of a star.	?

4 Which of the following belongs in the second column?

    A That was the style of building forts in the 1700s.

    B The shape let the fort be defended from all directions.

    C Many soldiers were needed to defend the fort.

    D It was the shape that best fit the land where it was built.

5 The fort was not well defended on the morning of May 10, 1775. What was a reason this was so? What was the result?

_____

_____

_____

_____

_____

_____

_____

6 Use a separate sheet of paper. Write a story about something going wrong in a funny way. Explain what goes wrong, why it goes wrong, and what happens because of it.

Unit 2 Reading and Writing for Information

Comparison and Contrast

When you read, you notice how things are alike and different. This can help you organize information in your mind. It helps especially when you're getting information from more than one place, or source. When you notice similarities between two things, actions, or ideas, you're **comparing.** When you notice differences between them, you're **contrasting.**

This diagram compares and contrasts two favorite animals:

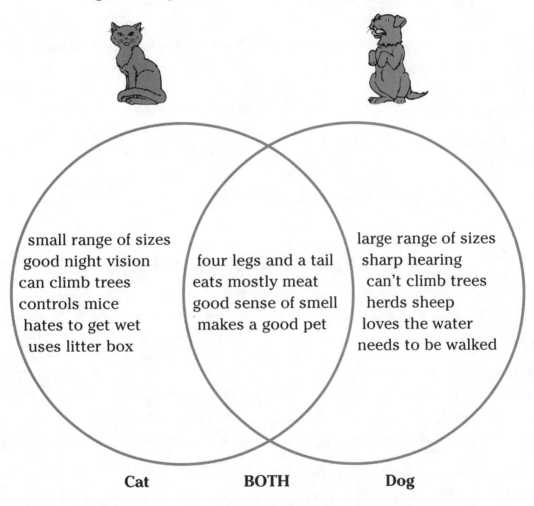

Cat	BOTH	Dog
small range of sizes	four legs and a tail	large range of sizes
good night vision	eats mostly meat	sharp hearing
can climb trees	good sense of smell	can't climb trees
controls mice	makes a good pet	herds sheep
hates to get wet		loves the water
uses litter box		needs to be walked

The middle of the diagram compares a cat and a dog. It shows how they are similar. The outer part of each circle contrasts the two animals. These circle parts show how a cat and a dog are different.

Guided Practice

Read these two selections about a basketball game. Notice similarities and differences between them. Then answer the questions that follow.

Raiders 11-0 After Latest Win

There seems to be no stopping the Cantonville Raiders. They crushed visiting Montlake Tuesday night, 57-42. It was Cantonville's 11th straight win this season.

Coach Jon Shulka's "no-star" lineup has a new star every game. This time guard Paul Tyndall came up big. He scored 23 points on eight-for-15 shooting. He wore out Montlake with his tough defense, breaking up the Tigers' game so that they seemed to lose control in the second half.

The Raiders took the lead 6-4 on center Ken Tugadi's dunk three minutes into the game. They never trailed after that. They put the game away with 11 straight second-half points, including six by Tyndall. Tugadi also had a fine game with 11 points and nine rebounds. Cantonville students and fans supported the team with non-stop cheering.

Old-timers are comparing these Raiders to the 1960–1961 state champions that went 26-0. But Coach Shulka laughs off such talk. "Tell me in March what our record is," he says. "Until then we'll play them one at a time." The Raiders next play at Falls City, Friday at 7:00 p.m.

Bad Sports in Cantonville

Anyone who saw our Montlake Tigers fall to Cantonville 57-42 Tuesday went home with a bad feeling. And it wasn't because of the score.

Yes, it's tough to lose, especially when you play a tight game against a fine team like the Raiders. But some Cantonville players and fans made it worse with their bad sportsmanship.

Someone should speak to Raiders' guard Paul Tyndall. Paul is a fine player. But his "trash talk" embarrasses the Cantonville program. Why won't Coach Jon Shulka put a stop to his disrespectful behavior? And why won't the officials step in? It's their job to control the game. They missed several foul calls against the Raiders' star. Yet they were quick to call fouls against the Tigers who were playing him close but clean.

Such behavior on the court brings out the worst from the fans. The home crowd never stopped screaming. They joined Raider players in taunting the visitors.

This is not the behavior we expect from our friends and neighbors. Any sports fan can admire a winning team. But maybe the Cantonville Raiders should take a long look at *how* they are winning.

Unit 2 Reading and Writing for Information

Which article reports the score of the game?

   A "Raiders 11-0 After Latest Win"   **C** both articles

   B "Bad Sports in Cantonville"   **D** neither article

> You can hardly believe that these articles are describing the same basketball game. Yet they both mention the same teams, and they both mention the score: 57-42. Choice C is the correct answer.

Which article calls it a "tight game"?

   A "Raiders 11-0 After Latest Win"   **C** both articles

   B "Bad Sports in Cantonville"   **D** neither article

> You can tell that the first article was written by a Cantonville supporter, while the second is by someone from Montlake. The first says that the Raiders "crushed" the Tigers. The second says that the Tigers played "a tight game" against the Raiders. Choice B is correct.

Which article contains mostly facts and details about the game?

   A "Raiders 11-0 After Latest Win"   **C** both articles

   B "Bad Sports in Cantonville"   **D** neither article

> If you want to know some details about how the game went, you wouldn't get them from the second article. It's an editorial. The first article gives you more of an idea about how players performed and why the Raiders won. Choice A is the correct answer.

Which article calls Paul Tyndall the star of the Cantonville team?

   A "Raiders 11-0 After Latest Win"   **C** both articles

   B "Bad Sports in Cantonville"   **D** neither article

> Both articles comment on Paul's play. But the first article says only that he "came up big" in this game. It describes Cantonville as having a "no-star" lineup. It's the second article that calls him the star of the team. Choice B is the correct answer.

Compare and contrast the two articles. What is similar about them? What is different?

_____

_____

_____

_____

_____

_____

_____

_____

Use a separate sheet of paper. Write an article describing a sports event or game you have seen or played in.

Test Yourself

Now read two articles about Mars and answer the questions that follow.

Article 1

What is it about Mars? The "red planet" has sparked more science fiction than any other place in space. Nearly 100 years ago, readers enjoyed Edgar Rice Burroughs' Mars adventure series. His Mars was imaginary. It had strange animals and towering cities. "Red" (good) Martians battled "green" (bad) Martians. Later came Ray Bradbury's gentle Martians and Robert Heinlein's wise Martians. And let's not forget H. G. Wells' scary Martians. Wells wrote *The War of the Worlds* in 1898. It was the first tale ever about "aliens" attacking Earth.

So why Mars? Maybe it's because people once believed that there *were* Martians. After all, Mars and Earth are practically in the same neighborhood of space. Parts of Mars could be warm enough to support life. The white caps at its poles grow larger and smaller with the seasons. Could they hold water? Parts of Mars sometimes look green through telescopes. Could there be plants there? And in 1877, an astronomer thought he saw water channels on Mars. "Canals!" the newspapers called them. People build canals. What sort of people built the ones on Mars?

The first spaceships visited Mars in the 1960s and 1970s. They sampled the soil and took pictures. There were no green areas. There were no canals. There were no Martians. There were no signs of life at all.

These discoveries pretty well ended science fiction about Martians—but not about Mars. In the 1990s, Kim S. Robinson wrote his *Mars* series. It's a story of people from Earth settling Mars. In these books, the first landing takes place in 2027. The first real human visit to Mars may take place about then.

Article 2

HOUSTON, November 23, 2004– Students have one more week to enter the Mars Rover Competition. In this contest, students in grades 3–8 design their own experiments. Then they build their own Mars rover models to perform them. The models must use simple supplies. Students may spend no more than $25 on them. The contest will be judged January 22 at the University of Houston.

Spirit: one of the Mars rovers

The competition is inspired by the real Mars rovers, *Spirit* and *Opportunity*. Both were landed on the Red Planet in January 2004. Their mission was meant to last three months. But they continue to send back data. They are controlled remotely by scientists on Earth. The rovers study Mars's soil, rocks, and craters. They are powered by solar energy.

There appears to be no life on Mars. The soil is poisonous. There is no liquid water. Radiation blasts the planet from space. But there are signs that Mars did have water billions of years ago. It sometimes gets as warm as a cool spring day on Earth. So it may have supported life long ago. The rover explorations may discover whether this is so.

Students in the rover competition read about Mars. They must consider the conditions on Mars in designing their models. The real rovers are studying these conditions to prepare the way for the first human landing on Mars. That may happen within the next 25 years.

1 What is the subject of **both** these articles?

   A exploring Mars

   B science fiction about Mars

   C people's interest in Mars

   D whether there is life on Mars

2 Which article describes the discoveries of the two Mars rovers?

   A Article 1

   B Article 2

   C both articles

   D neither article

3 Which article suggests that people may land on Mars within the next 25 years?

   A Article 1

   B Article 2

   C both articles

   D neither article

4 The president has proposed a program that would send people to explore Mars. Explain why you think this would be a good idea or a bad one. Use information from both articles.

   _____

   _____

   _____

   _____

   _____

5 On a separate sheet of paper, write a paragraph that answers the following questions. What do you think would be the most useful thing for science to discover? Why?

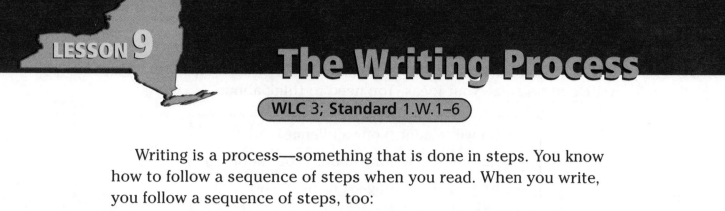

WLC 3; Standard 1.W.1–6

Writing is a process—something that is done in steps. You know how to follow a sequence of steps when you read. When you write, you follow a sequence of steps, too:

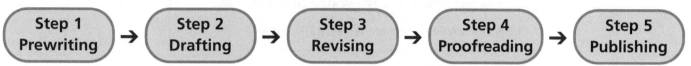

| Step 1 Prewriting | → | Step 2 Drafting | → | Step 3 Revising | → | Step 4 Proofreading | → | Step 5 Publishing |

If you follow the writing process step by step, your writing will flow more easily and make better sense. That's true whether you're writing a story or a single paragraph.

You follow the writing process when you're writing a long answer to a test question, too. On a test, you do some steps a bit differently than when you're writing for fun or for homework. The chart below shows the writing process for most test questions. You'll do better on tests if you follow the steps of the writing process:

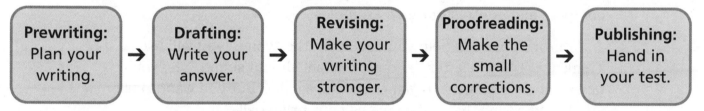

| **Prewriting:** Plan your writing. | → | **Drafting:** Write your answer. | → | **Revising:** Make your writing stronger. | → | **Proofreading:** Make the small corrections. | → | **Publishing:** Hand in your test. |

Follow these steps now to answer a kind of question you often find on tests. First, review the article about the game of Go on pages 27–28. Then read this test question.

> Suppose that you wanted to start a Go club at your school. The school rules state that all after-school clubs must be educational. Write a letter to your principal explaining why you think your school should have a Go club. Be sure to include:
>
> • an explanation of what Go is
>
> • at least three reasons why a Go club at school would be a good idea.

Step 1: Prewriting

Prewriting is planning. In this step, you think about what you will write and organize your ideas. You need to think about:

> • **who** will read it (your audience)
>
> • **what** you are writing about (your subject)
>
> • **why** you are writing (your purpose)
>
> • **what** you will say (your content)
>
> • **how** you will say it (your "voice")

On a test, some of these things are taken care of for you. Your audience is whoever will be scoring the test. The question tells you your subject—a Go club. It also tells you the form your extended response should take—a letter. You need to read the question carefully to be sure you understand the purpose for your writing.

Look for clues in the question that tell you what your purpose for writing is. This question tells you that you need to **explain** a game (give facts) and **persuade** the principal that it's educational (give reasons). Other questions may ask you to describe, summarize, compare and contrast, or give examples.

Your purpose can help you decide on the "voice" you will use. Think about how a letter to your principal should sound. Yes, you're talking about a game, and games are fun to play. But you want to use words and a tone that will convince your principal!

Now you need to think about content. What will you say that will describe the game and convince your principal to make it an after-school activity?

First, make sure you are clear about your main idea. Your main idea should summarize what the question is asking you to do. All the facts, details, and opinions you write should support this main idea. You probably want to write it down in a single sentence:

We need a Go club at our school.

A graphic organizer can often help you plan your content. For instance, in this question you need to include facts about Go and at least three reasons why the game is educational. You could use a **cluster map** or **web** to organize your facts and reasons.

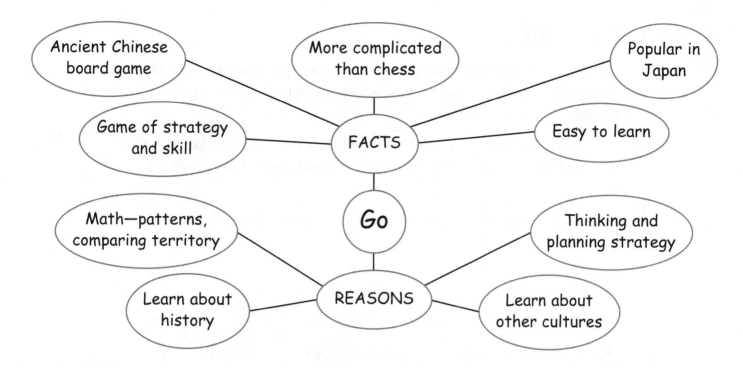

To plan other kinds of writing, you can use other graphic organizers:

• An **outline** or **note taking** helps you identify main ideas and supporting details.

> Facts about Go
> —Ancient Chinese board game
> —Game of strategy and skill
> —More complicated than chess

• A **timeline** helps you map out events in their correct sequence.

1755	1775	1908	1961
Fort Ticonderoga built	American Revolution	Fort restoration begins	Fort named National Historic Landmark

• A **Venn diagram** or **comparison chart** helps you compare and contrast information.

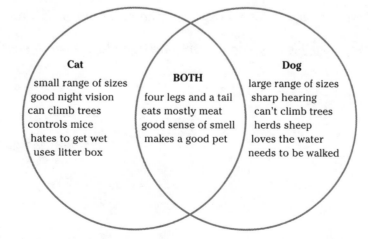

Step 2: Drafting

After you plan your work, you need to put your main idea and supporting details into sentences and paragraphs. This step is called drafting.

Drafting is where you do most of your writing. You'll make changes and corrections later. But in this step, you get your ideas down on paper.

Here is a draft of the prewriting plan made on page 71 to answer the question about the Go club:

Dear Ms. Campbell:

We have lots of clubs and activies after school. There's a chess club a computer club, and a math club. There are classes in spanish and French. There are sports clubs for basketball soccer, and track I think we need one more, a Go club.

Go is an ancient game of strategy and skill. It was invented in China more than 3,000 years ago. But its most popular in japan. Its played on a board with crisscrossing lines. You take turns placing stones where the lines cross to try capture territory. The winner gets the most territory. The rules are simple and easy to learn. A beginner can have a chance against an expert. It's my favorite game, and I think other kids would like it. Here are three reasons why Go is educational:

1.) You need thinking skills and strategy. 2.) You use math in planning how to capture territory and defending against the other player. 3.) You learn something about the history and culture and legends of other countries (Japan).

Sincerely,

Serena Baerga

Step 3: Revising

When you have finished your draft, you need to read it carefully and make changes to improve your writing. This is called revising. While you are drafting, you write down your own ideas. You think about what you know about the topic. While you are revising, you think about how it will look to your readers. You read your draft carefully and decide how you will change it to make it better.

When you revise, think about both the content and the organization of your work. Here are some of the questions you might ask yourself:

Content

- Does my writing have a main idea? Is it stated clearly enough for people to understand it?

- Have I included enough details? Should I add an important detail or an example anywhere?

- Have I included any unimportant details that I should have left out?

Organization

- Does everything I have included support my main idea and my purpose for writing?

- Are the relationships between my ideas clear? Do I need to add words, phrases, or sentences to help readers understand them?

- Are my sentences well written?

Imagine Serena Baerga is revising her letter about the Go club. The first thing Serena noticed was that her main idea wasn't clearly stated. It would be easy for Principal Campbell to miss the point. So she added a sentence at the beginning to make it clearer.

Serena thought she jumped too suddenly from explaining the game to listing the reasons why it is educational. So she made some changes in the second paragraph.

The next example shows how Serena's letter could be revised. See if you can figure out why each change was made.

Dear Ms. Campbell:

I'm writing to ask you to add a Go club to our after-school activies

program.

Our school has
~~We have lots of clubs and activies after school. There's~~ a chess club a

We have
computer club, and a math club. ~~There are~~ classes in spanish and French,

and
~~There are~~ sports clubs for basketball soccer, and track I think ~~we need one~~

~~more,~~ a Go club! (would be an excellent choice, too.)

Go is an ancient game of strategy and skill. It was invented in China more

than 3,000 years ago. But its most popular in japan. Its played on a board

Two players   **small counters**
with crisscrossing lines. ~~You~~ take turns placing ~~stones~~ where the lines cross

is the player who captures
to try capture territory. The winner ~~gets~~ the most territory. The rules are

simple and easy to learn. A beginner can have a chance against an expert. ~~It's~~

Go is a lot of fun to play. But it also improves your mind. It teaches you
~~my favorite game, and I think other kids would like it. Here are three reasons~~

~~why Go is educational:~~

~~1.) You need~~ thinking skills and strategy. ~~2.)~~ You use math in planning how

And
to capture territory and defending against the other player. ~~3.)~~ You learn

something about the history and culture and legends of ~~other countries~~

(Japan).

Sincerely,

Serena Baerga

Step 4: Proofreading

Now you have revised your work and are happy with it. The next step is to proofread it. Proofreading is for correcting mistakes. When you proofread, you make sure that:

- All words are spelled correctly
- Words are capitalized correctly
- Punctuation marks are used correctly
- Subjects and verbs agree
- Pronoun forms are right
- Titles are capitalized and in quotes

When you proofread, use these marks to show your changes.

Proofreading Symbols		
∧	Add letters or words.	This game is played ^on^ a board.
⊙	Add a period.	It is popular in Japan⊙
≡	Capitalize a letter.	two players take turns.
⌄	Add a comma.	You learn about history, culture, and legends.
/	Make a capital letter lowercase.	The Rules are simple and easy to learn.
ℓ	Take out letters or words.	We have the ~~board and~~ game.
∪	Switch the position of letters or words.	Use the stone white counters for the game.

Writers usually prepare a new, clean copy after revising and before proofreading. On a test, you probably won't have the space or time to do that. You have to proofread your revised answer and make changes with your pencil and eraser. Let's see how Serena's letter about the Go club looks after she proofreads her revision.

Dear Ms. Campbell:

I'm writing to ask you to add a Go club to our after-school ~~activies~~ activities program.

Go is an ancient game of strategy and skill. It was invented in China more than 3,000 years ago. But ~~its~~ it's most popular in japan. ~~Its~~ It's played on a board with crisscrossing lines. Two players take turns placing small counters where the lines cross to try to capture territory. The winner is the player who captures the most territory. The rules are simple and easy to learn. A beginner can have a chance against an expert.

Go is a lot of fun to play. But it also improves your mind. It teaches you thinking skills and strategy. You use math in planning how to capture territory and defending against the other player. And You learn something about the history and culture and legends of Japan.

Our school has a chess club, a computer club, and a math club. We have classes in spanish and French, and sports clubs for basketball, soccer, and track. I think a Go club would be an excellent choice, too.

Sincerely,

Serena Baerga

Step 5: Publishing

Publishing means making your writing public—sharing it with others. You can share your work with your friends or your family. You can post it on a bulletin board or include it in a class booklet. You can even post it on the Internet.

With a test, though, the publishing step is simple and quick. You just hand in your test paper!

Use the writing process to answer this question. First, read the question carefully. Use the space below for prewriting. Then turn the page to write your draft.

Imagine that you were going to spend a year on a remote island. You may bring two of your favorite games with you. They cannot be electronic or video games because there is no electricity on the island. There will be plenty of people to play with, but you will have to teach them the games. Write a letter to the people on the island describing the two games.

In your letter, be sure to explain

• why you chose those two games

• similarities and differences between the two games

• what makes the games fun to play

Prewriting

Drafting

Write your draft for the answer to the question on page 77.

_____

_____

_____

_____

_____

_____

_____

_____

_____

_____

_____

_____

_____

_____

_____

Revising, Proofreading, and Publishing

• Revise your draft to organize your writing on this page. Is your main idea clear? Do the facts and details support your main idea? Are your sentences well written?

• Proofread to check your writing for correct spelling, grammar, capitalization, and punctuation.

• To publish, write your final answer on a separate sheet of paper and hand it in.

Rubric for Test Questions

A rubric is a set of rules used to score writing. On a test, your writing might be given a score from 0 to 3, with 3 being the best. The people scoring the test use a rubric to decide your score.

Keep this rubric in mind as you work on your final draft for the test question on page 77. Rubrics may differ, but writing rubrics look something like this:

Score: 3	Score: 2
• Writing is strongly connected to the question.	• Writing clearly responds to the question.
• Strong, clear main idea identifies the theme.	• Reader can easily identify the main idea.
• Well-developed writing with well-organized ideas, examples, sequences, and conclusions.	• Writing is mostly well organized; may include some unimportant ideas. Examples, ideas, sequences, and conclusions make sense.
• Written in a lively voice with varied vocabulary and clear, complete sentences.	• Written mostly in clear and complete sentences with a good choice of words.
• Few or no errors in spelling, grammar, usage, capitalization, or punctuation.	• Some errors in spelling, grammar, usage, capitalization, or punctuation.
Score: 1	**Score: 0**
• Writing is connected to the question only in a general way.	• Writing does not seem connected to the question at all.
• The main idea is not clearly presented.	• There is no main idea.
• Writing is poorly organized. Ideas are incomplete and examples are not clearly connected; many unimportant details.	• Little or no planning or organization; few if any ideas presented; no connection between ideas and examples.
• Sentences use a limited vocabulary; may not be complete or may run together.	• Sentences make little or no sense, with poor choice of words.
• Many errors in spelling, grammar, usage, capitalization, and punctuation.	• Errors in spelling, grammar, and so on make the writing unreadable.

Editing a Paragraph

(WLC 3)

The fourth step of the writing process is proofreading. When you proofread, you find the mistakes and correct them. On reading tests, you may need to apply this skill to **editing a paragraph.** You are given a short paragraph that has a few mistakes in it. Your job is to find and correct the mistakes. You need to make sure that all sentences follow the rules of English. For example:

> • Verbs must have the correct forms and tenses.

       went   had
I ~~goed~~ to the zoo last Sunday. I ~~have~~ a great time.

> • Punctuation marks must be used correctly.

                       bears, lions,
I saw real grizzly ~~bears lions,~~ and kangaroos.

> • Pronouns must be used correctly.

They
~~Them~~ are some of my favorite animals.

> • All sentences should be real, complete sentences.

                   elephants and
I also like the ~~elephants. And~~ monkeys.

> • Capital letters should also be used correctly.

         I   zoo
I hope ~~i~~ can go back to the ~~Zoo~~ again soon.

Unit 2 Reading and Writing for Information

Guided Practice

This paragraph is a possible answer to question 4 on page 46. There are some mistakes in the paragraph. Correct the mistakes. Then look at the next page to see how well you did.

It must have been hard to live in america in the 1700s. There were no cars telephones, or computers. People did their cooking in fireplaces. They got around by horse and wagon. If they got sick, there is probably no doctor nearby. Most children went to one-room schools. Or didn't go to school.

Inside a one-room schoolhouse

It didn't take you long to find the first mistake, did it? "America" is the name of a place—a proper noun. It needs to be capitalized.

It must have been hard to live in ~~america~~ **America** in the 1700s.

What about the next sentence? There should be a comma after the word "cars."

There were no ~~cars~~ **cars,** telephones, or computers.

The next two sentences are okay. They need no corrections.

People did their cooking in fireplaces. They got around by horse and wagon.

What's wrong with the fifth sentence? It's about something that happened in the past. So the present-tense verb "is" does not belong.

If they got sick, there ~~is~~ **was** probably no doctor nearby.

One of the last two sentences isn't really a sentence. It's a fragment. Here is one way you could correct it:

Most children went to one-room ~~schools. Or~~ **schools or** didn't go to school.

Here is the whole paragraph again with all the corrections made:

It must have been hard to live in America in the 1700s. There were no cars, telephones, or computers. People did their cooking in fireplaces. They got around by horse and wagon. If they got sick, there was probably no doctor nearby. Most children went to one-room schools or didn't go to school.

Unit 2 Reading and Writing for Information

Test Yourself

Now follow the instructions for editing this paragraph.

Here is a paragraph a student wrote. There are some mistakes in the paragraph. Some sentences may have more than one mistake, and other sentences may contain no mistakes at all. There are <u>no</u> mistakes in spelling.

Read the paragraph and find the mistakes. Draw a line through each mistake in the paragraph. Then write the correction above it.

The Mohawk Trail was once a real trail. native Americans and settlers use it to travel between New York and Massachusetts. Now a highway runs along the route. They is very beautiful. Many people drives it to look at the scenery. But part of the old path is still there. Some people, choose to hike rather than drive. There is a place on the trail where you can see into four states. New York Massachusetts, Connecticut, and Vermont.

Cars travel along a winding Route 2, known as the Mohawk Trail.

When you write, you need to make every sentence count. Sometimes you need to make every word count. This is especially true on tests. You may need to answer a question with a short paragraph. You may need to write an answer that can fit in a graphic organizer. Here are some tips for writing these short responses:

- **Identify what the question asks you to do.** Are you being asked to find the main idea, summarize, or provide details that describe or explain something? Or does the question ask you to compare and contrast two things? Make sure you understand your purpose before you begin writing.

- **Plan your answer.** Note details in the selection that will help you answer the question. For example, if the question asks you why something happens, look for clue words that point to causes and effects. If you're writing a single sentence, find the most important detail that connects with the question.

- **Use strong, complete sentences.** Do not write fragments or run-ons. Make sure every sentence connects to the question.

- **Build paragraphs carefully.** The first sentence should clearly state the main idea of your answer. Each sentence that follows should contain details that support the main idea. You may want to end with a sentence that connects back to the main idea.

Guided Practice

In Lesson 3, you read an article about snow. Now read another article about a famous snowstorm and answer the questions that follow.

The Blizzard of '88

March 12, 1888, was a long-remembered day in New York City. On the evening before, a Sunday, there was heavy rain. It was driven by a strong northwest wind off Lake Ontario. After midnight, it turned to snow. By four o'clock Monday morning, it was taking just five minutes for the falling snow to erase footprints. Horse-drawn streetcars and wagons became stalled in the street. By 9:00 a.m., trains had stopped running. Snow clogged the switches, and the tracks were coated with ice. Many businesses never opened. Many people could not open the doors of their homes or shops. Some public schools were open in the morning, but all had shut down by afternoon.

Nothing could move. Horses and wagons were left in the streets. Telegraph and telephone wires were down. Electric power failed. In Brooklyn, the wind blew the roofs off houses. The Staten Island Ferry shut down after dark. Wind snapped the boats' flagpoles, and snow made it impossible for pilots to see. On city streets, people and horses were trapped in snowdrifts and died of cold and exhaustion.

On Tuesday morning, the shovels came out. Horse-drawn plows were useless. The snow had drifted six to fifteen feet deep. But New York began to dig out. And New Yorkers did not lose their sense of humor. Here and there, signs were stuck in the snowdrifts. They said things like, "Keep off the grass," "Do not pick flowers," and "Important notice: This is 23rd street!"

By Wednesday, the snow began to melt. People lit fires to help the sun do its job. Food began to trickle into the city. Communication with the outside world was restored. People began returning to work. By Friday the streetcars were running again, and people were able to see over the snowdrifts. Years afterward, anyone who had been there had a story to tell of the Blizzard of '88.

The snow on March 12, 1888, shut down New York City little by little. In the boxes below, write three things that the weather brought to a stop.

By morning...

_____

_____

_____

_____

By afternoon...

_____

_____

_____

_____

By evening...

_____

_____

_____

_____

You can easily identify this question as one that asks you to find a sequence of events. So you look for time clues in the selection. The first two paragraphs describe what happened on the day of the blizzard. You'll see words like "By 9:00 a.m.," "by afternoon," and "after dark." Here is one way you could fill the three boxes:

- By morning, the trains stopped running.
- By afternoon, the public schools closed down.
- By evening, the Staten Island Ferry shut down.

Unit 2 Reading and Writing for Information

People often think of a big snowstorm as something fun. Imagine that you had experienced the Blizzard of '88 and were telling someone about it. Would you describe it as fun? Explain why or why not.

_____

_____

_____

_____

_____

_____

This question asks you for your opinion. You need to find facts and details in the selection that will help you form and support your opinion. The main idea should be "The Blizzard of '88 was fun because..." or "The Blizzard of '88 was not fun because..." Details in the sentences that follow should support your opinion. The last sentence should sum up the main idea. Here is one possible answer:

The Blizzard of '88 was definitely not fun! We couldn't open our front door to get outside to play. We couldn't get to the store to buy food, but there wasn't any fresh food anyway because the trains couldn't bring it into the city. I felt sorry for those people in Brooklyn whose roofs blew away. I felt sorry for myself for all the shoveling I had to do. I like snow as much as anyone, but that was too much!

Test Yourself

In Lesson 8, you read two short articles about Mars. Now read another article about Mars and answer the questions that follow.

A team of astronauts leaves the habitat in their space suits. Around them is the dry, rocky Martian landscape. They are studying a crater that was formed by an asteroid that struck 23 million years ago. There are signs that water gushed out of the ground when it hit. The air is cold. The astronaut crew must be back inside before dark. Then the temperature will plunge well below freezing. But that won't happen for several months. Meanwhile, they have to watch out for polar bears.

Of course, there are no polar bears on Mars. The astronaut crew isn't on Mars either. They aren't really astronauts. They're scientists at a laboratory on Canada's Devon Island. It's called the Flashline Mars Arctic Research Station, FMARS for short. The scientists are experimenting with ways that people might someday explore Mars.

FMARS

Devon Island lies only 900 miles from the North Pole. It is a frozen desert, like Mars. Rain or snow rarely falls here. An asteroid really did land here long ago, wiping out most life. As on Mars, the summer temperature can get warm enough to go without a jacket. During the long Arctic winter, it drops to -70° F—about as cold as Mars's average temperature. The air here is good old Earth air, not Mars's thin, poisonous atmosphere. But wearing a spacesuit is practice for getting around on Mars. It also helps test new spacesuits for the real thing.

FMARS has been operating since 1996. The first crews camped out in tents but only for three weeks. Now there is a permanent habitat where scientists live for months at a time. They recycle all the water they use, as people will find no water on Mars. They bring with them all the food they need, as people will find no food on Mars. They experiment with ways that radio signals and computers might work on Mars. They perform experiments on rocks and soil, trying to discover areas where there might once have been springs of hot water. They built a robot that can float over the rocky ground and take pictures. Scientists on Mars will perform similar experiments.

The first people on Mars will face conditions much rougher than on Devon Island. They will be there for more than a year before they can return. There will be no helicopters to bring them out in case of emergency. But FMARS scientists are discovering and creating ways to explore the Red Planet. It's likely that the first Mars-bound astronauts will train for their mission here at FMARS.

1 According to the article, what are three challenges that the first people to reach Mars will face, and how will they face them? Write your answers in the boxes below.

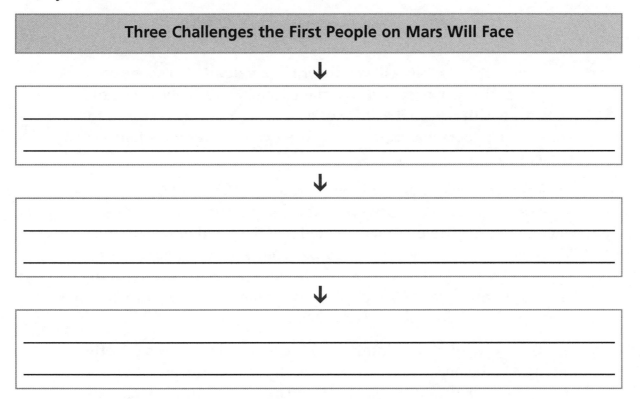

Three Challenges the First People on Mars Will Face

↓

_____

_____

↓

_____

_____

↓

_____

_____

2 Why was Devon Island a good site for the FMARS habitat? In your answer, use information from this article and from the articles in Lesson 8.

_____

_____

_____

_____

_____

_____

Some test questions ask you to write an **extended response**—an answer that is longer than one paragraph. You may be asked to explain something about a story or an article. You may be asked to write about a personal experience. When you answer questions like these, you're writing an **essay.**

When you write an essay, you need to use the writing process. In an essay, you may be dealing with several main ideas and supporting details. You have to plan an extended response and organize your ideas carefully. On a test, you may be given a planning page to do your prewriting. You may have two or more pages for writing your essay. Allow time for revising and proofreading if you want to get the best possible score.

Usually, the first paragraph of your essay will be an **introduction** that states the main idea. It should catch the reader's attention and make him or her want to read further. The next several paragraphs form the **body** of the essay. Each paragraph has its own main idea that supports the main idea of the essay. The last paragraph is a **conclusion.** It summarizes the ideas in the rest of the essay.

The other things to remember when you're writing an essay for a test are the same as when you're writing a short answer:

• **Identify what the question asks you to do.** Make sure you know your purpose before you begin writing.

• **Plan your answer.** You'll be responding to one or two listening or reading selections. Take notes as you listen. When you read, note details in the selection that will help you answer the question.

• **Use strong, complete sentences.** Make sure every sentence connects to the main idea of the paragraph.

• **Build paragraphs carefully.** Each paragraph should have a clear main idea. Each sentence in the paragraph should support the main idea.

Guided Practice

In Lesson 7, you read an article about a fish that was causing problems. Now read an article about a bird and answer the question that follows.

It seemed like a nice idea at the time. A man wanted to introduce to America all the birds mentioned in Shakespeare's writings. Around 1890, he brought 100 starlings over from Europe. He released them in New York City's Central Park. No one remembers this man's name. But his plan worked—at least for the starlings. Today there are about 200 million of them in the United States.

Some find the starling a pretty bird. Its black feathers shine with a purple gloss. They are tipped with cream-colored speckles. But starlings take over the nesting areas of woodpeckers, swallows, and other native birds. Their waste litters the ground and spreads disease. Flocks of starlings near airports cause airplane accidents. For these reasons and others, most Americans consider starlings pests.

It's no mystery why starlings are so successful. They eat almost anything. In some countries they are valued for eating harmful insects. But they eat helpful insects, too. They eat snails, frogs, worms, berries, and many kinds of fruit. They also eat farmers' crops and the feed farmers put out for their animals. When they find a good food source, they stick around. A flock of 1,000 starlings can eat a ton of cattle feed in a month. That's a *small* flock. Sometimes there are so many they look like a black cloud in the sky.

In the 1970s, flocks of 100,000 starlings were not unusual. They were causing huge amounts of damage and loss. That's when scientists, farmers, and the government decided that starlings had to be controlled. They have tried lots of ways. They trap and kill the birds. Farmers poison them. They spread nets over their fields and plastic over their animals' feed. Scientists bring peregrine falcons to starlings' nesting areas. These falcons feast on the smaller birds. In cities, people clear away wild plants that bear fruits, nuts, or berries. They scare starlings away with recorded noises.

None of these methods has been entirely successful. "Regardless of how we feel about starlings, they are very good at living in the environments we make," explains a bird scientist at Cornell University in Ithaca, New York.

Suppose that New York is having trouble with a kind of ivy. It was brought in from Africa to plant in people's gardens. Now it has spread out of control. It covers over and kills trees and other plants. Some people want the state government to bring in an insect species that does not live in New York. In Africa, the insect keeps the ivy under control by eating its roots. Write an article for a newspaper explaining why you think this would be a good idea or a bad one. In your article, use information from the article on page 91 and from the one on page 56.

In your article, be sure to explain

• how the starling and the Asian carp got out of control

• your thoughts about bringing in a new insect species to New York

• what other ways might be tried to control the ivy

Read the question again carefully. Then do prewriting. Take notes on both stories, writing down the important points. You may want to do a graphic organizer (Venn diagram) to compare and contrast information about the starling and the Asian carp.

The question suggests what your main idea should be:

It would be a good idea to bring in the insect because... Or:

It would be a bad idea to bring in the insect because...

The next step is writing your draft. The first paragraph should state your main idea strongly and clearly in a way that grabs a reader's attention.

The next few paragraphs should support the main idea. You need to explain *why* it's a good idea or a bad one using information from the two articles. Be sure to address the three points listed in the question. One paragraph might **compare and contrast** information about the Asian carp and the starling. Another might **draw conclusions** from that information to support your main idea. The next paragraph might **summarize** other possible ways to control the ivy, using information from the two articles and what you already know.

The last paragraph should bring your essay to a strong conclusion. In it, you might summarize the main ideas of the paragraphs and how they support the main idea of your essay.

After you write your draft, revise and edit your essay. Proofread it, checking for correct spelling, grammar, capitalization, and punctuation. Then write your final answer to the question on another sheet of paper. Here is a sample of a final answer:

Recently this newspaper printed an article about how African ivy is spreading out of control in our state. Some people say we should bring in an African insect to control the African ivy. I say, no way! Haven't they learned a lesson from the Asian carp and the starling? Bringing in a bug that doesn't live here naturally is a <u>bad</u> idea!

The starling is a bird that was native to Europe. Some were turned loose in New York City over 100 years ago. Now they are pests all over the country. The Asian carp is a fish. It was brought in to control algae and pollution. People thought they could keep it in fish farms, but it escaped. Soon it might be eating the food fish in the Great Lakes. How would people keep this African insect from escaping? Keep it in insect farms?

Both the starling and the Asian carp became problems because they eat all kinds of things. How do we know what this insect will eat? In Africa it eats ivy roots. Here it might find something it likes better. What will we do if this insect eats our food crops and garden plants?

There may be other ways to control the African ivy. Has anyone tried weed killer? What about sheep and goats? They eat all kinds of green stuff, including ivy. Maybe some kind of special fence would work. Or people could use shovels to dig up the unwanted plants.

Bringing African ivy to New York was a mistake. Bringing in another species that isn't natural here could be an even bigger one. Let the bugs go on eating African ivy in Africa. We should find another solution to our state's ivy problem.

Test Yourself

Read an article about a way of getting around in New York City and answer the question that follows.

See if you can answer this question: Where can a plane fly over a person who is walking over a car driving over a boat that is over a train? Here's a hint: It's in New York City. Another hint: It's a "place" that's also been called a work of art. Give up? It's the Brooklyn Bridge.

The Brooklyn Bridge crosses the East River. It connects Manhattan Island to Brooklyn. Until 1898, New York and Brooklyn were separate cities. The first ferry service between them began in 1642. New York was then a tiny Dutch settlement called New Amsterdam. The ferry was a rowboat. By 1802, dozens of boats were carrying thousands of passengers between the two cities each day. That's when people first started discussing the need for a bridge across the East River. It took another 65 years to come up with a plan to build one.

John A. Roebling was the engineer who made the plan. He designed a bridge that would be both useful and beautiful. It took more than 15 years to build it. Nearly 30 workers died from accidents during its construction. Among them was Roebling himself.

The Brooklyn Bridge opened to traffic on May 24, 1883. It was a day of celebration. Businesses closed in New York and Brooklyn. Bells rang in both cities. There was an hour-long fireworks display. More than 150,000 people walked across the 6,000-foot bridge that first day. They were joined by more than 1,800 horse-drawn vehicles.

Four bridges (and several tunnels) now connect Brooklyn with Manhattan. But there is "only one Brooklyn Bridge." Poems have been written about it. Great artists have painted it.

Unit 2 Reading and Writing for Information

John Roebling planned his bridge to be six times as strong as it needed to be. Was it? It still stands, while other bridges of its time were long ago taken down as unsafe. Roebling never saw an automobile. But nearly 150,000 cars cross his bridge every weekday. Another 4,000 people cross on foot or on bicycles. And while there was a three-cent toll in 1883, today people cross absolutely free.

Hundreds of feet down, below the East River, are the tracks of the New York City subway. That's the train that runs under the boat under the car....

Imagine that you have a cousin coming to visit from another country. You will be spending a few days together in New York City. Your cousin is interested in seeing historic sights. He has sent you an e-mail asking whether it would be interesting and fun to walk across the Brooklyn Bridge. Write a letter to him answering his question. Use information from this article.

In your letter, be sure to

- explain why walking across the bridge would (or would not) be interesting and fun

- describe some of the things he would see and experience

- give some details about the bridge

Use the space below for prewriting. Then use the next page to write your draft. Revise, edit, and proofread your letter. Remember to check your writing for correct spelling, grammar, capitalization, and punctuation. The last step is to write your final answer on a clean sheet of paper.

Use the space below to write your draft.

Unit 2 Reading and Writing for Information

Unit 3: Reading and Writing with Literature

There are two kinds of things to read—information and literature. Literature is the reading that you do for entertainment and enjoyment. It includes stories, poems, and plays. In this unit you will learn about all of these.

To talk about literature (and to answer some test questions) you need to know some special vocabulary. You will learn the important terms that people use to talk about literature in lessons 13–20 of this unit.

13 Story Elements   Good stories have a setting, point of view, theme, characters, dialogue, plot, and conflict. You will learn how to recognize these elements of a story and use them to write stories of your own.

14 Story Structure   In this lesson you will learn how stories are put together, from beginning, to middle, to the end.

15 Making Reading Connections   The literature you read at school is usually fiction. Some stories are realistic fiction, or stories that are like real life. You can connect them to your own experiences. You also read fables, fairy tales, and folktales. The characters are not real and the story is made up. Knowing what kind of story you are reading helps you make connections to your own life or to something else you have read.

16 Making Predictions   When you watch a television program, you are probably guessing what will happen next. That's true when you're reading, too. Making good predictions shows that you can follow the action in a story and that you understand what is happening.

17 Inferences and Conclusions   Sometimes the author doesn't tell you everything in a story. You have to put together the facts or details to make inferences and draw conclusions about the story's characters or events.

18 Figurative Language   In this lesson you will learn new ways that words can be used.

19 Poetry and Plays   Poems and plays have very specific structures. You need to be able to recognize them and understand how they make the play or poem work.

20 Writing About Literature   When you write about literature, you have to pay attention to story elements and structure and all the skills you learned in lessons 13–19. Plus, it's important to use good writing skills. This lesson will guide you through writing a story and extended responses to questions about literature.

Story Elements

You want to tell a friend about a story you just read. Where will you begin? With your favorite **character** and the things he says? Maybe you want to explain the **plot.** That's what happens in the story. Or should you start with the **setting?** That's where the story takes place and what it's like. All these elements work together to make a good story. It may be a folktale or a legend. It may be realistic fiction, a fantasy, or a tale set in historical times. Whatever kind of story it is, it will have these elements.

Characters make the story real. An author usually describes how characters look and talk. The "talk" part is called **dialogue.** The way a character talks can be as important as what he or she says.

The **plot** means the events or action of the story. They usually take place in a time sequence. (This is called *chronological* order.) The plot also includes a **conflict.** Sometimes the conflict is a struggle between characters. Or, it can involve two ideas. For example, a plot can involve a character's inner conflict about doing what is right or wrong.

The **setting** is the time and place in which events of the story happen. The time can be past, present, or future. It can be a certain year, time, or season. An author uses the setting to create the mood, tone, or feeling of the story.

Unit 3 Reading and Writing with Literature

Guided Practice

Read this selection. Then answer the questions that follow.

"Hey girls, what's up?" Graham had come into the backyard.

"Socks is," Tisa said, pointing. "He got into the McFaddens' yard. Then he tried to get back over the fence by climbing the tree."

"Only instead of crawling out a branch and jumping down, he kept climbing higher," I explained.

Graham peered up at Socks. He laughed. "He's sure got himself stuck."

"Couldn't you climb up our ladder and get him?" I said.

"I'm not *that* tall, Carly," he said. "Besides, we can't go into the McFaddens' yard while they're away."

"We should call the fire department," Tisa suggested.

"You got that from one of your old picture books, didn't you?"

"Uh-huh."

"Firefighters did that in Grandma's day," Graham said knowingly. "They don't any more. At least not without the city charging a lot of money. There's nothing we can do. Socks will come down when he's hungry enough. They always do."

Tisa seemed about to cry. "Maybe Mom and Dad will think of something," she said.

"They won't be home for hours," I said, gazing at Socks. While we were talking, he had climbed several branches higher. Now he was above the level of the third-floor porch off my bedroom. He was meowing away. "It will be dark soon."

"So he'll spend the night up there," Graham said. "It won't hurt him. Next time he'll know not to climb trees."

I was thinking. I looked at the two boards leaning against the back fence. I eyed the distance between my bedroom porch and poor Socks sprawled on the high branch. I thought about the crutches Graham got when he hurt his knee playing football.

"Do you know where Mom keeps that roll of heavy tape?"

"Sure, in the kitchen drawer," Graham said. "Why?"

"I have an idea," I said. "I'll need a good pair of scissors and some old cardboard cartons."

"What are you going to do, Carly?" Tisa asked.

"I'm going to build Socks a ramp."

What is the setting of this story?

A a farmhouse in the country

B an imaginary world

C a big-city apartment building

D a family's backyard

The setting is the time and place where a story happens. This story seems to be taking place outdoors. The first paragraph tells about Graham coming into the backyard. There is another family's yard on the other side of a fence. The realistic setting and tone tell you we're not in an imaginary world. Choice D is the correct answer.

What time of day does the story take place?

A early in the morning

B around lunchtime

C late in the afternoon

D at night

Carly points out to her brother and sister that "It will be dark soon." So you know that choice C is correct.

Unit 3 Reading and Writing with Literature

The main conflict in the story is between

A the kids and Socks

B Socks and the tree

C Carly and her brother and sister

D Carly and the problem of Socks in the tree

The plot of this story is centered on a problem: How are the kids going to get Socks out of the tree? You could say that Socks is in conflict with the tree. But the story is more about the kids than about Socks. Carly isn't really in conflict with her brother. She just sees that a problem needs to be solved. Graham thinks it will solve itself. The last few paragraphs show you that choice D is the correct answer.

In this selection, Carly can best be described as

A kind and generous

B strong and fearless

C quiet and respectful

D clever and resourceful

Carly may be all of these things. But the plot of the story has her finding a solution to the problem of Socks in the tree. She has a plan to rescue the cat by using some odd materials. She's good at thinking of ways to do things. Choice D is the correct answer.

What does Graham's dialogue tell you about the kind of person he is? Use examples from the story in your answer.

_____

_____

_____

_____

_____

_____

Every story is told from a **point of view.** Sometimes one of the characters tells the story in his or her own words. That is called **first-person point of view.** The character uses first-person pronouns such as *I* or *we*. A story can be told from the **third-person point of view.** Then the narrator uses third-person pronouns such as *he, she,* and *they.* The previous story has a first-person point of view—Carly's.

A story also has a **theme.** The theme is the topic or subject of a story. It is not the same as the plot. In the previous story, the plot can be summarized as "Carly rescues Socks from the tree." The theme may be described as "children solving problems," or "pets," or "family life."

Now read a selection from another story and answer the questions that follow.

There was the usual joking around as we left the gym. It had been a good practice. I was tired, but it was the pleasant feeling of having worked my body well. Coach Rich had praised me for my defense. He'd had good things to say about all of us. So while I was waiting for Dad, I was surprised to hear Cole's voice raised in anger.

"He may be a friend of yours, but he's no friend of mine," Cole said. He was talking to Ethan Tajima. "If he's invited to your birthday party, I'm not going!"

I saw Ethan draw back from Cole as if from a blast of heat. "Hey, what's that about?" he said. "Since when isn't Ben your friend?"

"Since I changed schools," Cole said sourly. "He's in my face every time I see him. He's like, 'Aren't you too *gifted* to hang with us?' As if I had any choice about where my parents send me."

"So you can be in the same house with him for a couple hours, can't you?" Ethan said. "We'll eat pizza. We'll watch a movie. We'll play video games. You don't have to hug and kiss him."

"Yeah, let me know if he gets the flu and can't come," Cole said. "Then I'll be there."

I spoke up. "Doesn't Mike Rosen go to Warren now?" That was Cole's school, the one you had to pass a special test to get into. "I mean, I know he does."

"Yeah, so what?" Cole spun on his heel to face me.

"He's still friends with Ben. I see them together all the time."

"Mike's friends with everyone. It's a talent of his. He's going to be school president next year." Cole kicked a pebble on the sidewalk. "Maybe Ben doesn't hassle him. Or maybe he doesn't mind it. I don't know, and I don't care. All I can tell you is if I've got to listen to any more of Ben's stuff, I'm going to take boxing lessons first."

"Hey, Cole," Ethan sounded funny. "You're my friend. Ben's my friend. You've been at all my birthday parties since I was six. Adam too," he said, with a nod at me. "I'm supposed to choose between you now all of a sudden?"

"I see Ben every day." I was trying to be helpful. "I never hear him say anything bad about you. Maybe you're wrong about him."

"And maybe you should stay out of this!" Cole screamed in my face. "I'm sorry," he added quickly. "I'm not mad at you, Adam. You just don't know."

"It's okay, don't sweat it," I said. "Here's my dad," I added, seeing his car approaching. "I'll talk to you guys later." I had the idea of making peace between Ben and Cole. But as my dad pulled up to the curb, I thought of something I'd once heard him say: Never get in the middle of somebody else's fight.

This story is told from

   A   Adam's point of view

   B   Cole's point of view

   C   Ethan's point of view

   D   third-person point of view

> The narrator in this story uses the pronoun "I," so you know the point of view is first person. Cole and Ethan are both "he," so you know that it's Adam who is narrating the story. The correct answer is choice A.

The selection suggests that the theme of the story is

   A   sports

   B   friendship

   C   birthday parties

   D   life in the big city

> The story is about a conflict between friends and how it is resolved. Cole's anger at Ben is hurting Ethan and threatens to ruin his birthday. Adam is trying to decide whether to try to make peace between his two friends. The story may include elements of all the answer choices, but it's about friendship. Choice B is correct.

What are some words or phrases that describe Cole?

_____

_____

_____

_____

_____

On a separate sheet of paper write a story about a conflict that you once had with another person, or about one that you tried to "patch up."

Unit 3 Reading and Writing with Literature

Test Yourself

Now read part of another story and answer the questions that follow.

The gate stood alone at the top of a little hill. It lit up the night as brightly as a fast-food restaurant. As they came near, a monster rose slowly out of a hut and stood barring their way.

The mammoth came to a stop before the gate. "It's a toll gate," he whispered. "Give him a coin."

Jack held out a piece of gold. The monster just looked at it. "Put it away," it growled in a voice like a truck engine. "Make me laugh or go back where you came from."

"He means a joke," Tusker said. "Sometimes the toll isn't money. You never know what they'll ask for."

The monster didn't look like it had any sense of humor. Jack couldn't tell whether it was a dinosaur or a road-building machine. Its green leathery skin looked painted on. It had long ears like a donkey. It had four arms that ended in metal tools. It had big rubber tires instead of feet. The pouch hanging from its belly looked like a giant shovel.

Jack leaned over Tusker's shaggy head. "What kind of jokes does it like?" he whispered.

"What do I know about jokes?" Tusker said. "I'm a prehistoric mammoth."

"But you know this place! You brought me here!"

"Oh, right, now it's <u>my</u> fault!" the mammoth whined. "Look, you wanted someone who isn't afraid of monsters. So you picked me. You want jokes, next time bring a cartoon character."

"All right, all right," Jack said. The monster was waiting. Something really silly from the first grade, Jack thought. "Why did the chicken cross the road?" he said.

"To get to the other side," the monster said. "Not funny."

"Jack, that's so old it's a fossil!" Tusker hissed.

"I thought you didn't know anything about jokes," Jack said.

"Well, I remember hearing that one back in the Stone Age."

Jack tried again. "Why did the little turtle walk softly?"

"I give up," the monster said.

"Because he couldn't walk, hardly," said Jack.

"Right," said the monster. "What's a turtle?"

"Don't you know any good ones?" Tusker whispered hoarsely.

Jack wondered how many tries he had, but three seemed a likely guess. He took a deep breath. "What do you do when your toes get stuck in the mud?" he said.

"I give up."

"Call a toe truck."

"Call a toe truck," the monster repeated. It broke into a smile. A sputter escaped its leathery lips. Its enormous belly shook. "A toe truck. That's a good one! Haw, haw, haw, haw, haw, haw, HAW!"

The monster stepped aside. The gate lifted. Jack urged Tusker forward, and together they passed through the gate into Zorgoland.

1 What is the point of view of the story's narrator?

A first person point of view

B third person point of view

C the monster's point of view

D Tusker's point of view

2 What is the setting of this selection?

A on another planet

B in an imaginary land

C on an American highway

D in a long-ago time

3 The conflict in this selection is between

    A Jack and Tusker

    B the monster and Tusker

    C Jack and the monster

    D Jack and his feelings

4 The theme of this selection is best described as

    A a test of courage

    B solving a problem

    C fantasy and fun

    D making new friends

5 Tusker's dialogue suggests that he is

    A brave but complaining

    B wise but clumsy

    C smart but shy

    D grumpy but kind

6 How would you describe the monster? Base your answer on his dialogue and on the narrator's description.

_____

_____

_____

_____

_____

_____

7 Use a separate sheet of paper. Choose one of your favorite stories. Describe its setting, theme, and point of view. Explain what the main conflict is in the story.

Story Structure

Standard 2.R.10; 2.W.4, 8

Every story has a beginning, a middle, and an end. When you read a story, you understand it better if you recognize these parts.

> • In the **beginning** of a story, you meet the main characters and find out what the conflict is going to be about.
>
> • The **middle** of the story contains most of the action. It leads up to the high point, or **climax,** of the story.
>
> • The **end** of the story starts with the climax. This is where you find out how the conflict turns out. You know by then whether the story will have a happy ending or a sad one. After that, there may be some final action showing what happens to the characters.

Even a very short story has these three parts. For example, think of "The Tortoise and the Hare." The beginning of this story introduces the characters. It leads up to the tortoise challenging the hare to the race. By then you know something about the characters and what the conflict is about.

The middle of the story is about the race itself. The characters act like the way they were introduced in the beginning. The tortoise goes on in his slow, steady way. The boastful, foolish hare lies down to take a nap.

At the end of the story, the climax comes. The tortoise wins the race. The hare (and you) are left to think about the lesson of the story.

BEGINNING

MIDDLE

END

Unit 3 Reading and Writing with Literature

Guided Practice

Read a folktale from Norway, a country in northern Europe. Then answer the questions that follow.

The Big White Cat

Once upon a time, a hunter captured a large polar bear. As it was the Christmas season, he decided to take it to the king as a gift. It so happened that he was crossing the mountains on Christmas Eve. He came to a cottage where a man named Halvor lived. He asked if he and his bear could stay for the night.

"Bless us, but you cannot," said Halvor. "Every Christmas Eve, trolls come and drive me and my family out. We'll have no shelter for ourselves, let alone a guest."

"Oh?" said the hunter. "If that's your worry, then please let us stay. I can sleep in the storeroom, and my bear can sleep under the stove."

Well, he argued so long that Halvor finally agreed to let him stay. Halvor and his family left. But first, they set the table for the trolls. There was bread and fish and sausages and a big Christmas pudding.

No sooner had they left than the trolls came in. There were big ones and small ones. There were trolls with long tails and trolls with no tails. There were trolls with big, long noses. They ate and drank and made a great mess.

Then one young troll saw the bear lying under the stove. "Here, kitty, want something to eat?" he said. He took a piece of sausage and poked it against the bear's nose. It was hot. The bear woke up. It rose with a growl and chased all the trolls outside.

The next day, the hunter and his bear went on their way. A year later on Christmas Eve, Halvor was expecting the trolls again. He was out chopping wood when he heard a troll call to him from the forest.

"Halvor!" cried the troll. "Do you still have that big white cat?"

"Yes," Halvor called back. "She's lying at home under the stove. She now has seven kittens, all bigger and fiercer than herself."

"Then we will have our Christmas feast somewhere else!" said the troll. And the trolls never bothered Halvor or his family again.

The "beginning" of this story ends when

    A   the hunter captures the bear

    B   the hunter comes to Halvor's house

    C   Halvor tells the hunter about the trolls

    D   the trolls come into the house

> Even a story as short as this one has a beginning, a middle, and an end. The beginning takes us to the point where we know what the story is about. At first, we think it is going to be about the hunter. But it really is about Halvor and the trolls. That's the conflict—Halvor against the trolls. Choice C is the correct answer.

The climax of the story comes when

    A   Halvor and his family leave food for the trolls

    B   a young troll thinks the bear is a cat

    C   the bear chases the trolls away

    D   a troll tells Halvor they will eat somewhere else

> Choices A, B, and C are events in the *middle* of the story. Even after the bear chases the trolls away, you can't tell for sure how the story will turn out. The climax comes when we learn that Halvor has "won" his conflict with the trolls. Choice D is the correct answer.

The end of the story explains how

    A   the hunter presented the bear to the king

    B   the trolls never bothered Halvor again

    C   the bear had seven large cubs

    D   the trolls came back the next Christmas

> Remember that the end of a story starts with the climax. In folktales, what follows the climax is usually something short and simple. In this story, the "end" is contained in the last paragraph. Choice B is the correct answer.

Write a summary of "The Big White Cat." Make sure that you include details from the beginning, middle, and end of the story.

_____

_____

_____

_____

_____

On a separate sheet of paper, write a short story about a funny holiday experience. Make sure it has a beginning, a middle, and an end.

Test Yourself

Now read another story and answer the questions that follow.

It was a hot day in June. Laci sat on a bench in the park, watching Ian in the wading pool. She fanned herself with a magazine. Before her, little kids were laughing and splashing. Behind her, kids her age were playing kickball. She wished she were someplace cool. Ana and Misa were at the movies with Ana's older sister. They had asked her to come, but she was stuck minding Ian for the day.

A bee buzzed around her head. Laci tiredly waved it off.

"It's my vacation too," she had complained to her mom. "Why can't _I_ have some fun for a change?"

"Laci, I have to work, and someone needs to be with Ian this week until Tot Camp starts," her mother said. "You'll have your fun days, too."

"Ouch!" Laci said suddenly. The hot, stabbing pain in her arm told her at once she'd been stung. She swatted at the bee angrily with the magazine. Only it wasn't a bee. It was a large black hornet.

Suddenly the air was filled with buzzing. There were three hornets flying around the bench. No, four. Laci jumped up, her arm throbbing. She looked up. A crumpled ball of gray paper hung from a nearby tree. But it wasn't paper. It was a hornets' nest. Hornets were flying in and out. One high kick from a kickball player could knock it loose.

She looked at the kids playing happily in the pool. "Ian, get out of the pool!" she called to her brother.

"No!" Ian called back.

"I'll get you some ice cream!"

"No!" Ian yelled happily. "I'm having too much fun!"

Later, Laci would remember what happened only in pieces. She took her brother firmly by the arm and led him from the pool. "Wait right here," she ordered. Then she turned to the nearest adults, two young women who were watching their kids. "There's a hornets' nest on that tree," she pointed. "Please help me get the kids out of the pool."

"Oh my goodness!" one woman said. Someone screamed. Then everyone was moving quickly.

"Someone tell those kickball players to stop," Laci called. She wondered why everyone was so excited. There's no real danger if the nest isn't knocked down, she thought. It isn't like a building is on fire.

Then she saw a park supervisor hurrying toward her. Laci waved. She talked. She pointed. The supervisor looked. "Everybody, clear the park," he called calmly. "Clear the park now! Please. Yes, you! Thank you!" Only then did he pull out a cell phone and punch in a number.

Later, Laci and Ian watched from the supervisor's office as a green truck pulled up. A woman got out. She wore a white suit, gloves, and a mask. She climbed a ladder and quieted the hornets with chemicals. Then she cut down the nest and put it in a box in the back of her truck.

"We owe you our thanks," the park supervisor told Laci. She and Ian were eating ice cream cones. "Stinging insects cause a lot of people to panic, but you kept your head."

"Maybe I was just mad because they'd already got *me,*" Laci said. She held up her arm. The place where she had been stung was red and swollen. "May I please have an ice cube?"

Unit 3 Reading and Writing with Literature

1 The beginning of this story is over when

    A Laci gets stung

    B Laci sees the hornets' nest

    C Laci calls to Ian in the pool

    D Laci leads Ian from the pool

2 Which of these events takes place in the end part of the story?

    A Laci and Ian eat ice cream.

    B The park supervisor appears.

    C Laci tries to stop the kickball game.

    D People run screaming from the hornets.

3 At the climax of the story, we know that

    A Laci is finally going to have fun on her vacation

    B Laci's arm is red where she was stung

    C no one else is going to get stung

    D Ian isn't going to get out of the pool

4 Describe in order three things that happen in the middle part of the story.

    _____

    _____

    _____

    _____

    _____

    _____

5 Use a separate sheet of paper. Choose a story that you know well. Explain what happens in the beginning, the middle, and the end. Use no more than two sentences for each part of the story.

Making Reading Connections

Standard 2.R.4, 5, 11, 12; 2.W.5

You're always **making connections** when you read. A sentence, a character, or a place reminds you of something you already know. Usually, you don't have to read very far to tell whether a story is nonfiction (true) or fiction. But some fiction is realistic. If you read a story about kids in a family or in school, you can connect the story's happenings to things in your own life. Or if you read a book set in New York in the 1700s, you know that cars and telephones would be out of place. And you know that people are people. Their ways are different, but their thoughts and feelings are just like ours today.

Suppose you're reading a fable, such as "The Tortoise and the Hare." You probably know people like the hare. That's why you laugh knowingly when the tortoise wins the race. And you can tell that the lesson is "slow and steady gets the job done."

Knowing what kind of story you're reading helps you make connections and understand many things. For example, if a story has animal characters that act like people, you know that it's probably a fable or a folktale. Fables and folktales often teach a lesson or try to explain why things happen.

Fairy tales sometimes teach a lesson, too. But fairy tales have a quality of magic about them. They often have imaginary characters like giants, witches, and elves. Many fairy tales begin with "Once upon a time…" and end with "…and they lived happily ever after."

Legends like "The Adventures of Robin Hood" are stories from the past about people, places, and events. You can connect them to a particular time and place in history. A hero, like Robin Hood, is usually the main character.

A.D. 1190 England
The Adventures of Robin Hood

Heroes in legends have adventures like these.

Guided Practice

Read part of a story and answer the questions that follow.

The Rabbit's Crop of Money
A story from Central Africa

It was the beginning of the rainy season, and time to plant the gardens for the year. So Great Chief called all the animals together. He asked what each would grow. Antelope said she would grow rice. Monkey said he would grow melons. When it came Rabbit's turn, he said, "I will grow money."

"Whoever heard of growing money?" asked Great Chief.

"If you give me a bag of money for seed, I will show you how it's done," said Rabbit.

So Great Chief gave him a bag of money. At once Rabbit went off and spent it. He bought clothes, food, and beads for himself. While the other animals worked, Rabbit spent the year being lazy.

At harvest time, all the animals brought in the food they had grown. "Rabbit, where is your crop of money?" Great Chief asked.

"Money grows slowly," Rabbit said. "It has barely sprouted."

Rabbit spent several more months enjoying himself. After a while Great Chief sent for him again. "Rabbit, where is your crop of money?" he demanded.

"It grows well," Rabbit said. "It is just beginning to flower."

This went on for some time. Finally Great Chief sent Pig to Rabbit's house. "Great Chief wants me to see your money garden and report back to him," said Pig.

Now, long before this Rabbit had known he was in trouble. When you tell one lie, it nearly always leads to another. He said, "Pig, it would have been foolish to plant a money garden near the village. Everyone would try to steal it. I have it hidden away in the jungle."

"Then you will lead me to it," said Pig.

Now Rabbit felt in worse trouble than ever. What was he going to do? They set out into the jungle and walked and walked. Then Rabbit said, "It is a long way to the money garden. We will have to spend the night there. Let me go back and get my pillow."

Rabbit ran back a little way. Then, creeping close to where Pig stood waiting, he took a reed and blew a blast like a horn. "Father, here is a wild pig!" he called in a deep voice. "Bring your spear quickly so we can kill him."

This kind of story is **most** like

A nonfiction

B a legend

C a fairy tale

D a fable or folktale

Because of the talking animals, you know this story isn't true or nonfiction. The story has no heroes or magical qualities, so it's not a fairy tale or legend. Did you recognize that this story is leading up to a lesson? That tells you it's a fable or folktale, choice D.

The lesson this story is probably trying to teach is about

A where lying can lead

B not wasting your money

C working hard to store up food

D respecting the power of a chief

Stories like this usually teach a lesson about human behavior. Which of Rabbit's behaviors got him in trouble? You can guess by his actions that he respects the chief's power. He was lazy, and he did waste the money Great Chief gave him. But it's his lying that got him in trouble. You can also guess that it will lead to more trouble. Choice A is correct.

In a story like this, you would **not** expect to meet a

A lion

C hunter

B policeman

D queen

You probably know that there are lions in Africa, so you could meet a lion. A hunter or a queen would not be out of place either. But police officers belong to modern times and real places. Rabbit may find himself in trouble, but it's not likely that a policeman will arrest him. Choice B is the correct answer.

Make connections to other stories you have read that are like this one. What do you think is likely to happen in the rest of this story?

_____

_____

_____

_____

_____

On a separate sheet of paper, write your own fable that teaches a lesson. Give it a modern setting and characters.

Test Yourself

Now read part of another story and answer the questions that follow.

"Well, Ms. Woodswoman, where are we?"

Jenny jiggled her compass. She trained the flashlight on her map. She shook her head. "We're right in the middle of nowhere, Andy."

"Oh, what a relief!" said her brother. "For a minute I thought we were *lost.*"

"Hey, it's not my fault," Jenny said. "The compass broke. That's probably because you stowed it next to the steel hatchet," she added accusingly.

"Is that so?" Andy said. "Well, lucky for us, I thought of something you didn't." He held up the bag of trail mix. It was nearly empty.

"I've been marking the trail from the campground," he said proudly. "We'll be able to find our way back before dark."

"Andy, the birds and ground squirrels will have eaten every raisin and every nut by now! And that's all we had to eat for ourselves!"

They stood glaring at each other in the gathering darkness.

"Help me gather some fallen branches," Jenny said. "I'm going to build us a shelter and dig a fire pit. We may be here all night."

"How lost can you get in a state park?" Andy tried to sound brave. "Mom and Dad will tell the park rangers. They'll find us."

"Sure they will, but maybe not until morning."

"Wait a minute, what's that?" Andy pointed deep into the woods.

"Bears! Wolves! Big Foot! Come on, Andy, go get some branches!"

"Cut it out! I see a light! Hello!" Andy shouted. "We're here! Hello!" Before Jenny could stop him, he took off into the woods.

"Andy, get back here!" Jenny shouted. "You're supposed to stay in one place! If you run away, you'll get really lost!"

But her brother didn't answer. Jenny had no choice but to take off after him. Now she saw the light, too. Someone with one of those big lantern-type flashlights, she thought with relief. She heard branches breaking as Andy plowed through the woods. The light grew brighter. Jenny came to the edge of a clearing where Andy stood staring. When she saw what was in the clearing, she stopped and stared, too.

"It's a shopping mall!" she said in wonder. "A mall here in the middle of the woods—full of lovely things to buy!"

"Are you crazy?" Andy said. "Anyone can see it's a video arcade. Just look at all those cool games!"

"Welcome, children!" said a soft voice. An old woman stood in the clearing, beckoning to them. "Come on in and have some fun!"

1 Which of these things from the story is something imaginary and not real?

    A   two children lost in a state park

    B   birds and squirrels eating the trail markers

    C   a boy running deeper into the woods

    D   the kids see different things in the clearing

2 Which of these is **most likely** to happen at the end of this story?

    A   The kids will have an adventure on another planet.

    B   A kindly woodcutter will return the kids to their parents.

    C   The kids will have a funny adventure with the old woman.

    D   The kids will spend a scary night in the shelter Jenny builds.

3 How is this story similar to one you have read or heard? How is it different?

_____

_____

_____

_____

_____

_____

_____

4 On a separate sheet of paper, tell about a fiction book or story that you have read that is true to "real life." How can you connect it to things that happen in your life?

Making Predictions

Standard 2.R.6

As you read, you make guesses about what is most likely to happen in a story. Guessing ahead is called **making a prediction.**

You often make predictions as you read. A title helps you predict what a book or a chapter will be about. After you read the first few paragraphs, you should be able to predict whether the book will be fiction or nonfiction. Thinking about what you're reading and what you already know helps you make good guesses about what will happen.

© The Continental Press, Inc.   Do not duplicate.

Guided Practice

Read the first part of a story and answer the questions that follow.

Mystery of the Old Trunk

Chapter 1
Summer People

When I heard that the Old Sneyd Place had been sold, I had to go down and check out the people who had bought it.

The Old Sneyd Place had stood in our town since before it was a town. The original stone house was built in 1740. Generations of Sneyds had added onto it over the years. The house had stood empty since old Miss Lucy Sneyd died. That was when my dad was a kid. He and his sisters had explored its dark rooms. They had played pretend adventure games in the weed-grown front yard. And so had I.

Now that was over. Boards had been taken off the windows. Gardeners had made the yard look pretty. A work crew had repaired the old stone wall. The dirty gray house had been painted a cheerful brown and yellow. And a family named Simons was moving in.

I was prepared not to like Ben Simons even before I met him. I saw him trailing after his parents. He was struggling with a cardboard box that he was bringing in from a van. He had Rich City Kid written all over him. "They've got one kid?" I'd said when Dad told me about the Simonses. "Why does a family that small need a house that big?"

"They're turning it into a bed-and-breakfast," Dad said. "A kind of hotel. They're hoping to attract people on vacation from the city."

Great, I thought. Summer people here year round. Just what our town needs.

Ben Simons looked like summer people, all right. He was about 10 years old, my age. He would probably be in my class at school. He was a small kid with dark hair that fell over his eyes. He saw me looking at him from behind the wall. We nodded to each other. I know I should have offered to help him carry stuff in. Be a good neighbor. Meet his family. But that wasn't how I was feeling just then.

"Hi, I'm Greg," I called. "Anyone tell your family about the ghost?"

Ben looked at me. Then he set down the box and walked over my way. "Ghost, huh?" he said. "You saying this house is haunted?"

"A girl named Elizabeth Sneyd drowned trying to row across the Sound," I said, repeating the local legend. "It was in the Revolutionary War. She was trying to warn people that the British were coming. They say you can see her walking around with a lantern some nights."

Which of these clues does **not** help you predict that this story will be fiction?

A the title of the book

C a house that was built in 1740

B a ten-year-old telling the story

D the picture that goes with the story

The title itself suggests fiction. The picture and the fact that a child is telling the story should convince you that it is "only a story." Choice C is correct.

The "mystery" in the title will probably be about

A how Elizabeth Sneyd died

C whether or not the ghost is real

B a robbery at the old house

D something hidden in the house

There is an old house and the title suggests that the mystery involves an old trunk. So, it's probably about something that happened a long time ago, but we know how Elizabeth died and we know that ghosts aren't real. Choice D is the correct answer.

Which of these will **most likely** happen in the story?

A Ben and Greg will end up being friends.

B Ben and Greg will travel back through time.

C Greg will be trapped in the house with a ghost.

D Ben's family will sell the house and move back to the city.

This seems like a realistic story, not fantasy or science fiction. You don't expect the ghost to be "real" or that the boys will travel through time. You've probably read enough fiction, though, to predict that Ben and Greg will become friends and be involved in solving the mystery together. Choice A is correct.

A later chapter is called "The Clue in the Attic." What might happen in that chapter? Base your prediction on what you have read so far.

_____

_____

_____

_____

_____

Test Yourself

Now read another part of the story and answer the questions that follow.

Sunlight spilled across Water Street. Summer people strolled by, looking like people do on vacation. They walked slowly. They paused at the windows of the antique shops on their way to the beach.

"I'm not supposed to bother the guests," Ben explained. "After I help serve breakfast, I'm supposed to be outside or in our part of the house. So it would be hard to tell my parents what I saw."

"What did you see?" I asked impatiently.

"Well, this Ms. Holden—Judy Holden—she was tapping the walls and measuring them with a tape measure. When she saw me standing there, she must have jumped three feet! But she just gave me a big fake smile and said it was interesting the way these old houses were constructed." Ben stopped to catch his breath.

"She asked for the Old Colony Room when she checked in," Ben added. "Maybe there was a reason she wanted to be in the oldest part of the house. I think she's looking for something!"

"Look, there she is!" Ben grabbed my arm and pulled me into the doorway of The Pelican's Feast. A young woman was coming out of the town library. She was dressed for the beach, in yellow shorts and a straw hat. But her face was all business. As she turned down the street, she pulled a cell phone from her bag and made a call. "Does she look like someone on vacation to you?"

"Ben, lots of people stay in touch with their jobs while they're here. I bet she's got a computer in that bag, too."

"But no books—because she wouldn't have a town library card! What else is in that library?"

"Magazines. Videos. A meeting room. One room's kind of a museum of the history of the town. There's a—"

"Greg, that's it! She was checking old records—about our house!"

"I tell you, some people just think old stuff is cool. That's one reason they come to a town like ours instead of Fire Island."

Ben hopped up and down. "Let's follow her," he said. He ran a few steps out into the street. Then he dashed back. "You follow her," he said. "She knows me. She won't recognize you, Greg."

"Ben, listen, I think you're making a—"

"Follow her!" he insisted. "See where she goes. Please!" A car slammed on its brakes as he ran across the street toward the library.

1 What do you think Greg will do next?

    A He will follow Judy Holden.

    B He will tell Ben he's being foolish.

    C He will go home and forget the whole thing.

    D He will tell Ben's parents about his strange behavior.

2 In the library, Ben will probably

    A check out some books to read

    B look at the museum of town history

    C try to find out what Ms. Holden was doing

    D tell the librarian to watch out for Ms. Holden

3 Judy Holden will **most likely** turn out to be

    A just a woman on vacation

    B a long-lost relative of the Sneyd family

    C an author writing a book about the town's history

    D someone who is searching for something in the old house

4 What do you think is going to happen as this story continues? Base your prediction on both selections.

_____

_____

_____

_____

_____

5 On a separate sheet of paper, write a paragraph that tells part of an exciting story. Then trade papers with a classmate. Predict an ending for each other's stories.

Unit 3 Reading and Writing with Literature   **125**

Inferences and Conclusions

In stories, just as in nonfiction, a writer does not state every fact plainly. Writers assume you can figure out some details based on what you know and what you are reading. This is called **making inferences.**

It was a gray, rainy day. Going up a steep hill, our school bus made a funny sound. The driver, Mrs. Ennis, quickly put on the flashing lights and stopped the bus. A police car pulled up, and the officer guided traffic around the bus.

The story says:
The bus made a funny sound.

You know:
Cars or buses should not make funny noises.

You can infer:
There was something wrong with the bus.

When you put pieces of information together, you are **drawing conclusions,** or **making generalizations.**

Eric's shoes crunched on the newly fallen snow. He wove his way along the crowded sidewalk. Across the street, trees in the park were dark and bare under their white blanket. But on this side, store windows were bright with colored lights and shiny packages. Holiday music poured out of every door.

The story says:
It's snowing. The trees are bare. There are colored lights and holiday music.

You know:
Snow and bare trees are seen in winter. You see decorations and hear music like that before Christmas.

You can conclude:
This story takes place in December.

Guided Practice

Read this selection. Answer the questions that follow.

It was the first really warm day of the year. On such a day you could actually believe that summer would come again. There was a mood of celebration. Nobody wanted to come in off the playground. No one could concentrate on verbs or long division. Finally Mrs. Leary took pity on us. She let us have the last half hour of the afternoon as extra recess. I think she was glad to be outside, too.

After school, Meade Street was as full of moms and kids as on a Saturday in July. Bikes were brought up out of basements. Girls played hopscotch and jumped rope. I played stoop ball with Carl Ianelli and the Marcus twins. We played last fall's World Series between the Dodgers and the Yankees, only this time the Dodgers won. We talked about the real Dodgers. They would be opening at Ebbets Field in two weeks. We were all sure that this was The Year.

No one paid attention to the truck at first. "Holtz Electronics," it said across the back. Since the war ended, everyone seemed to be getting new things. There were new sofas and new refrigerators. There were new radios and new Victrolas for listening to the latest music. We had won the war. Our dads were working. Times were good and getting better. There were always empty crates for little kids to play in. Otherwise, someone getting a box delivered was no big deal.

Except this one was. By twos and threes, kids left their play. Moms broke off their talking. They hurried down the block, babies and all, to the building where the truck stood. When we heard what had been delivered to the Selmans, our game ended. Everybody on the block knew everybody else. Nobody thought it was rude to push into the Selmans' apartment to have a look.

I'd seen them before, but only in store windows. It was an enormous box made of dark wood. An antenna like a pair of rabbit's ears sat on top. Tubes glowed red through holes in the back. There was a screen that was about as wide as a kid's spread-out hands. A pattern of slanted horizontal lines sizzled on it. The man from Holtz Electronics turned some knobs. He moved the antenna. The lines snapped into a picture. It was a woman holding up a box and talking. Everything was in gray and white and black.

Everyone cheered. Then we shushed each other so we could hear.

You can conclude that this story takes place in

A   spring

B   summer

C   fall

D   winter

The narrator tells us that it was the first warm day of the year. Later we find out that the baseball season will begin soon. From these clues, you can conclude the story takes place in spring. Choice A is the correct answer.

Mrs. Leary is probably

A   a neighbor

B   the narrator's mother

C   the narrator's teacher

D   a woman who repairs TV sets

Mrs. Leary is mentioned in the first paragraph. This paragraph takes place at school. You can infer that because the narrator mentions recess, verbs, and long division. As Mrs. Leary allowed them "extra recess," you can conclude that she is a teacher. Choice C is correct.

Information in the selection suggests that the story is

A   a folk or fairy tale set "once upon a time"

B   a fantasy set in an imaginary world

C   a realistic story set in the present day

D   a realistic story set in time gone by

In this story kids go to school, ride bikes, live in apartments, and talk about sports. So you can infer that it's not a folktale or a fantasy. Yet the narrator has never seen a TV set before except in store windows. These facts let you infer that the story is taking place in the past. (In fact, it's 1948.) Choice D is the correct answer.

You can conclude that this story will mostly be about

A a family's funny adventures

B how TV leads to changes in a neighborhood

C programs of television's early days

D games children played in earlier times

The Selmans' new TV set is clearly the focus of the story. People on the block drop what they're doing to check it out. You can conclude that it's the first TV set on the block. You know how television fits into people's lives today. You can infer that in a few years, most families on this block will have one. So choice B is correct.

What are some inferences and conclusions you can make about life in the time and place where this story is set?

_____

_____

_____

_____

_____

Test Yourself

Now read another selection and answer the questions that follow.

Long shadows were falling across the sidewalk when Sammy came home. He didn't come on his own this time, though. A man brought him in a car.

"Are you the Reynosos?" he called.

"I'm Amber Reynoso, and that's our dog!" I said happily. I could see that Sammy was happy, too. "Thank you so much for bringing him back! Where did you ever find him?"

"In my backyard," the man said. "He was digging up my garden."

"Oh," I said. Uh-oh, I thought.

The man got out of the car. "Are your parents home?" he asked.

"I'm Rafael Reynoso," Papa said, coming out of the house. He walked heavily down the porch and across the grass to the curb. "Thanks for bringing the dog back. Sorry about the damage. The fence hasn't been built that can keep this guy in."

"It's more of a problem than 'sorry' can solve," the man said. "He tore up my prize shrubs."

"Don't worry, I'm good for it," Papa said. "Let me give you the number of my insurance guy. I've got it inside." He trudged back into the house.

"Couldn't you please let my dog out while you're waiting?" I asked the man. Sammy had his face pressed up against the back window of the car.

"With pleasure," the man sighed. He pushed a button in his car. The back sprang open. Sammy bounded out. He showed in his usual way how happy he was to see me. "I guess I don't need to ask why you don't keep him indoors," the man said.

"We're lucky the man likes dogs," Papa said. It was after dark. We were sitting around the kitchen table. Papa had called a family meeting to discuss the Sammy problem. "He was actually nice, considering what Sammy did to his flowers. What's going to happen next time?"

"We've got to build a stronger fence," my brother Cesar said.

"Yeah, out of what?" said Papa. "Concrete blocks and razor wire? You want our house looking like a war zone?" His eyes rested on me. "I hate to say it, but I think we need to give Sammy away to someone in the country."

"Papa, no!"

"If you've got any other ideas, honey, let's hear them."

"You know, Tina at school was telling me about her neighbor who's a dog trainer," said my sister Maggie. "Ms. Beale claims she can make any dog a good dog."

"Sammy is a good dog!"

"Yeah, well this Ms. Beale is really supposed to understand dogs. The way Tina tells it, she was born with four legs and a tail."

"Yeah?" Papa looked doubtful that anyone, human or dog, could understand Sammy. "Well, see if you can find out her phone number."

1 The main problem the Reynosos have with Sammy is that he

  A bites people

  B keeps running away

  C annoys people with his barking

  D buries things in other people's yards

2 How does Amber let you know that this passage begins in the early evening?

  A She tells you that shadows were long.

  B She tells you that she had just finished supper.

  C She tells you that Sammy had been gone all day.

  D She was outside when the man brought Sammy home.

3 When Papa says "Don't worry, I'm good for it," he means that he will

  A go to the man's house and fix his garden

  B take Sammy to Ms. Beale for training

  C make sure that Sammy won't bother him again

  D make sure the man gets paid for damage to his garden

4 How do you think the man knew the Reynosos' name and where to bring their dog? Explain how you made this inference.

  _____

  _____

  _____

  _____

  _____

5 Maggie's friend says that Ms. Beale "was born with four legs and a tail." This is supposed to mean that she really understands dogs. On a separate sheet of paper, write an expression like this to describe someone who is good at fixing things. Write another to describe someone who is good at music.

Unit 3 Reading and Writing with Literature   **131**

Figurative Language

Standard 2.R.14; 2.W.1.b; 2.W.4

Sometimes writers use special words or phrases to create pictures in your mind. This special language is called **figurative language** or figures of speech. For example, you may have heard someone say, "That horse can run like the wind." This gives you more of a picture of how fast the horse runs rather than just saying, "That horse runs fast." This lesson will help you think about how writers use language and how you can use language to create pictures in your own writing, too.

Here are some of the figures of speech that writers use.

> You have learned about one figure of speech, **idioms.** An idiom is a phrase that has a meaning apart from the words in the phrase. For example, we say that someone "came down with a cold." *Came down with* is an idiom that means "became ill." It has nothing to do with the usual meanings of *came* or *down.*

> When you say that a pillow is "as hard as a rock," you are using a **simile** (SIM-uh-lee). A simile compares two things that are very different using the words *like* or *as.* It helps you understand something in an unusual way. "The wind tapped like a tired man" is an example of a simile from a poem.

> If you compare things without using *like* or *as,* you are using a **metaphor** (MET-uh-for). "It's raining cats and dogs" is a metaphor. It tells you that the rain feels as heavy as animals falling from the sky.

> **Personification** is another kind of comparison. The writer makes something that is not human seem like a person in some way. "A breeze sang through the trees" is an example of personification.

Unit 3 Reading and Writing with Literature

Guided Practice

Read this story about 17-year cicadas. Then answer the questions that follow.

The Buggiest Year
by Lia Chen

As insect plagues go, I suppose it's pretty mild. They don't bite or sting. They don't eat farmer's crops. And they only show up in huge numbers every 17 years around here. But I hope I'm still living in the city in 2021 when the next brood of cicadas hits New York.

I remember 1987. I was 10 that spring. We lived across from a wooded lot in Kingston. One morning we woke up to a scratchy screeching noise. It was as loud as a chainsaw.

"Oh, no, the cicadas are here!" my mom said.

Their invasion was like a horror movie—only this was real! Swarms of big bug-eyed insects had decided to settle down in our neighborhood. The unwelcome guests kept up their chatter, day and night. You could close the windows, but that didn't shut out the noise. You couldn't talk on the phone or watch TV. The noise drove us bonkers, especially my poor dog. When you went outside, you'd see a black cloud of cicadas rising up from the ground. They're clumsy fliers, so they'd bump into you. To avoid being bugged, I wore my brother's football helmet and my swimming goggles when I went outside. The cicadas only hung around for a few weeks, but those were the longest weeks of my life. Then they died—all over the place. We shoveled them up into mountainous heaps.

In 2004 I was lucky. By then, I was living in the city. We only saw a few cicadas here and there. Their screeching was drowned out by traffic noise. That's why I hope I'm still in the city in 2021. Or maybe by then I'll move to Arizona or someplace else where cicadas don't go.

Which of these phrases from the story is a metaphor used to describe the cicadas?

A a black cloud

C bug-eyed insects

B in huge numbers

D like a horror movie

> Find each of these phrases in the story. Which one compares the cicadas to something without using *like* or *as?* Near the middle of paragraph 4, a sentence says that outdoors you'd see a black cloud of cicadas rising up from the ground. So "a black cloud," answer A, is a metaphor used to describe the cicadas.

What simile did the author use to describe the noise of the cicadas?

A insect plagues

C a scratchy screeching

B kept up their chatter

D as loud as a chainsaw

> A simile compares things using *like* or *as.* The last sentence in paragraph 2 says that the noise of the cicadas was "as loud as a chainsaw." The correct answer is D.

The author uses personification by comparing the cicadas to

A clumsy fliers

C unwelcome guests

B the longest weeks

D mountainous heaps

> At the beginning of paragraph 4, the cicadas are compared to noisy people who come as guests to a neighborhood. These "unwelcome guests" settled down and "kept up their chatter." Answer C is correct.

Write a sentence that uses the word "bugged" as an idiom. Explain what your sentence means.

_____

_____

_____

_____

_____

Unit 3 Reading and Writing with Literature

On a separate sheet of paper, write a paragraph about your favorite animal or insect. Use some figures of speech to tell why you like this creature.

Test Yourself

Now read a selection from another story and answer the questions that follow.

"You're looking as pleased as punch," Colin's mother commented.

"I ought to be," Colin said. He put his feet up on the desk and closed his eyes. "I just aced Ms. Connor's math test." He gestured with his head at the piece of paper that lay on a corner of the desk. His mother picked it up and examined it.

"Well, this is wonderful!" she said. "Just last week you seemed completely in the dark about fractions!"

"But all the studying I did really paid off," said Colin. "The test was a piece of cake. I think math and I are going to be friends from now on." He looked at his mother as though taken with a sudden thought. "Hey, Mom," he said. "Since I've really changed my study habits, how about an extra hour of TV tonight?"

His mother shook her head as she returned the paper to the desk. "Nice try, Colin."

1 Which of these is a metaphor that Colin uses to describe the test he took?

    A a friend

    B a piece of cake

    C a piece of paper

    D a sudden thought

2 In paragraph 2, Colin says that he aced Ms. Connor's math test. This means that he

    A didn't do well

    B doesn't like his teacher

    C got an 'A' on the test

    D has trouble with fractions

3 Which of these things is made to seem like a person in the selection?

    A Colin's desk

    B the test paper

    C math

    D TV

4 "In the dark" is an idiom that means

    A afraid to learn

    B studying all night

    C working without a light

    D without understanding

5 Find two other figures of speech in the selection and tell what each of them means.

_____

_____

_____

_____

_____

6 On a separate sheet of paper, write a paragraph about something you can do well. Use some figures of speech to describe what you do and how well you can do it.

Poetry

Poetry uses musical language to create word pictures and sound effects in your mind. As you read a poem, think about these elements.

Many poems repeat sounds at the ends of words. This is called **rhyme.** Sometimes the rhyme comes at the ends of a line of poetry:

> *The sun does arise*
>
> *And make happy the skies*

Sometimes the rhyming words appear in the same line:

> *There was a little girl who had a little curl.*

Most poems have a pattern of stressed and unstressed beats in a line. This is called **rhythm.** A stressed beat has more force than an unstressed beat.

> *The **sea** is **calm** to**night***

Sometimes a poem repeats the same (or similar) beginning consonant sounds in a line. In this line, the hard *c* sound is repeated:

> ***C**ake, **c**ookies, and **c**andles at the **c**lose of day*

Some poems use words that sound like what they mean:

> *The **clanging** of the bells, the **meowing** of the cats*

Every poem has a **speaker.** The poem takes the speaker's point of view.

Guided Practice

Read a poem and answer the questions that follow.

Bed in Summer

by Robert Louis Stevenson

In winter I get up at night
And dress by yellow candle-light.
In summer quite the other way,
I have to go to bed by day.

I have to go to bed and see
The birds still hopping on the tree,
Or hear the grown-up people's feet
Still going past me in the street.

And does it not seem hard to you,
When all the sky is clear and blue,
And I should like so much to play,
To have to go to bed by day?

The speaker in this poem

   A   is afraid of the dark

   B   likes winter better than summer

   C   can't fall asleep because it's too noisy

   D   doesn't want to go to bed when it's still daylight

> You probably figured out that the speaker is a child. He mentions "the grown-up people's feet." He has to go to bed when someone tells him to. The speaker compares getting up in winter, when it's still dark, to going to bed in summer, when it's still light. "The sky is clear and blue." He'd "like so much to play." And yet it's bedtime! Choice D is the correct answer.

Which line in the poem suggests that it wasn't written recently?

A And dress by yellow candle-light.

B The birds still hopping on the tree,

C And does it not seem hard to you,

D To have to go to bed by day?

This poem was written in the 1800s. Then as now, birds hopped on trees, and children hated to be sent to bed when it was still light outside. Homes, however, were not lit by electricity. In winter, people dressed by candlelight. Choice A is the correct answer.

In each stanza of this poem

A all four lines rhyme

B none of the lines rhyme

C the first line rhymes with the third and the second with the fourth

D the first line rhymes with the second and the third with the fourth

Like many poems, this one is divided into **stanzas**—groups of lines separated by spaces. In the first stanza, *night* rhymes with *light* and *way* with *day*. The other stanzas keep the same pattern. Read the poem carefully, and you'll see that choice D is the correct answer.

Which of these lines would best fit the rhythm of the poem?

A I wish I didn't have to go to bed early.

B A bird's nest outside my window

C The shouts of children in the park

D People are calling to me from the street.

Any one of these lines might fit the subject or the feeling of the poem. But only one fits the rhythm. Speak any line of the poem out loud, for instance: "I **have** to **go** to **bed** by **day.**" Do you hear where the stressed and unstressed beats fall? Only one answer choice fits that pattern, choice C.

What word pictures and feelings was the author trying to create in this poem? Explain your answer.

_____

_____

_____

_____

On a separate sheet of paper, write your own poem. Have it describe a feeling that you think children a hundred years from now will share.

Test Yourself

Now read these poems and answer the questions that follow.

A Slash of Blue
by Emily Dickinson

A slash of Blue—
A sweep of Gray—
Some scarlet patches on the way,
Compose an Evening Sky—
A little purple—slipped between—
Some Ruby Trousers hurried on—
A Wave of Gold—
A Bank of Day—
This just makes out the morning sky.

Eastern Shore Dawn
by Erik Fargo

As marsh reeds rustle,
Tenting some silent swimmer—
One watchful heron.

1 Which of these lines would best fit the rhythm of "A Slash of Blue"?

A The green grass and the brown hills

B The grass is green below the sky of blue.

C The sky is colorful at sunrise.

D A streak of green, a patch of brown

Unit 3 Reading and Writing with Literature

141

2 Which word in "Eastern Shore Dawn" sounds like what it means?

A rustle

B tenting

C swimmer

D watchful

3 In "A Slash of Blue," the poet compares the sky to a person

A dancing

B just waking up

C putting on clothes

D finding hidden treasure

4 Who is the speaker in each of these poems? Explain your answer using details from the poems.

_____

_____

_____

_____

_____

5 On a separate sheet of paper, write your own poem. Have it include sounds that add to the meaning or the feeling of the poem.

142 **Unit 3 Reading and Writing with Literature**

Plays

A **play** is a story that is performed by actors on a stage. A play is divided into **acts,** as a book is divided into chapters. Acts may be divided into **scenes.** A scene is part of the action that takes place in one place. Whether you watch a play or read one, it has acts and scenes.

Characters are the people who have parts in a play. A list of these characters is called the cast. It always appears at the beginning of the play or in the program. In a theater program, the name of the actor who plays each part follows the character's name. Sometimes there is a **narrator** who describes events in the play to the audience or reader.

The **setting** is the time and place where the action of the play happens. Sometimes the setting is described in a brief **introduction** at the beginning of a play. This introduction gives the reader background information about the characters and events in the play.

Stage directions explain how actors should move and speak. In a script, these stage directions are usually printed in *italics* and set off from the characters' names and the dialogue.

Dialogue is the words characters speak in a play. In a **script,** or printed version of a play, dialogue comes directly after the character's name. A **monologue** is a long speech spoken by one character to the audience.

Props are objects, such as books or telephones, that are used by the characters on a stage. **Scenery** is the backgrounds and larger objects that create the setting of the play. **Lighting** refers to the types of lights used on stage and how bright they are. The props, scenery, and lighting are usually described in the stage directions.

Guided Practice

Read this scene from a play. Then answer the questions that follow.

Fourteen Ways of Becoming a Lion

by Risa Knight

The Cast

Philip Rowles, *a fourth-grade student*	Aidan Roberts
James Rowles, *his father*	Neal Jackson
Lucy Rowles, *Philip's 13-year-old sister*	Cerise Callender
Sunday Ideyami, *an 8th-grade student*	Robert Ikoh
Grace Ideyami, *Sunday's mother*	Maria Galindez

ACT ONE Scene One

The living room of the Rowles family apartment. The lighting suggests early evening. A door is at right. At center is a table piled with books, papers, and a backpack. At left, PHILIP ROWLES is playing a video game. We hear game sounds under his dialogue.

Philip: *(excitedly)* Got you! *(pause)* Come on, come on, come on!

Philip suddenly freezes. Then he turns off the game machine and stuffs it back in the TV cabinet. Now we hear what he hears—someone coming up the stairs. Philip closes the cabinet quickly and dashes to the table. He bends over his homework just as his father, JAMES, comes through the door.

Philip: (*pretending to be busy*) Hi, Dad.

James: (*putting down a briefcase*) Hi, Phil. How was school?

Philip: Okay, I guess. How was work?

James crosses to the TV cabinet, opens it, and puts his palm on the screen. He frowns at Philip, who pretends not to notice.

James: Too much of it. But I can get off early enough Friday to go to your game.

Philip: (*without feeling*) That will be great, Dad.

James: You get your math test back today?

Philip: Yes.

James: Well?

Philip: (*glumly*) What do *you* think?

James closes the cabinet. He crosses to the table and sits down next to Philip.

James: Philip, you're a smart boy. You shouldn't be having so much trouble with math.

Philip: (*not looking at his dad*) Yeah, well, tell that to my teacher.

James: I'm telling it to you. (*sharply*) Philip, look at me! (*Philip, startled, looks angrily at his father.*) Philip, I've decided to get you a tutor.

Philip: What for?

James: What do you think? To help you do better at math.

Philip: I don't need any help.

James: I think you do. (*pause*) Sunday Adeyami will be tutoring you on Tuesday evenings and—

Philip: (*interrupting*) Sunday Adeyami? That clown upstairs?

James: —Saturday afternoons after basketball practice. And you won't start off by calling him names! He's in Lucy's class at middle school. She says he's good in math and great at explaining things.

Philip: What kind of a name is Sunday anyway? It's a day, not a name!

James: Maybe he'll tell you if you ask him. You'll be seeing him tomorrow evening at seven in his apartment. *(He rises from the table.)* Excuse me, I have to cook supper before your sister gets home.

James exits left. Philip looks after him for a moment.

Philip: Great.

Lights fade to black. End of ACT ONE Scene One

What does the stage direction in this line tell a reader?

Philip: *(without feeling)* That will be great, Dad.

A	the look on Philip's face	**C**	the way Philip speaks
B	the way Philip walks	**D**	what Philip is thinking

The stage direction doesn't say anything about movement or how he looks. The way the actor says the line *reflects* what the character is thinking. But the stage direction is only concerned with how the actor speaks the line. Choice C is correct.

What is an example of a prop used in this scene?

A	a door	**C**	the stage lighting
B	a backpack	**D**	Philip's voice

A prop is an object that can be moved or carried by an actor. The door is part of the scenery, not a prop. Choice B is the correct answer.

What is an example of dialogue that is spoken by James?

A "You get your math test back today?"

B *James closes the cabinet.*

C "What kind of name is Sunday anyway?"

D *Lights fade to black.*

Choices B and D are in italic type. They are stage directions. Choice C is dialogue spoken by Philip. Choice A is the correct answer. It is dialogue spoken by James.

Unit 3 Reading and Writing with Literature

How do Philip's dialogue and stage directions give an actor ideas about how to play the character? Use details from the script in your answer.

_____

_____

_____

_____

Test Yourself

Now read this scene from a play and answer the questions that follow.

Ms. President

The Players:

Narrator	Daniel Purifoy
Danae Sutherland, *a fourth-grade student*	Shira Marcus
Jenny Singer, *a fourth-grade student*	Melissa Miller
Jake Hannigan, *a fourth-grade student*	Rob Archer
Tommy Wu, *a fourth-grade student*	Jason Bing
Ms. Winterbottom, *a school-board official*	Sharon Edelweiss
Mr. Hallstrom, *a music teacher*	Tarik Farshad

Students, parents, and school-board members

ACT ONE Scene One

A single spotlight on the NARRATOR. He wears an Uncle Sam costume.

Narrator: Hello, my fellow Americans. You probably wonder why I'm here. Well, this is a play about democracy. I'm always on hand when Americans get together to make choices for themselves. Here's a secret for you—*(leans forward as if whispering)* They don't always agree! Yes ma'am, freedom can get a little noisy. Sometimes people rise up off their sofas and yell, "That's unfair!" Sometimes people have different ideas about what "fair" is. That's when I have to be… *(He pulls a catcher's mask from the shadows and puts it on.)* an umpire. Sometimes I take a few hits myself! *(He begins to stroll slowly* *offstage right.)* But the game goes on. Right now, it's about to get going on a school bus, somewhere in the great state of New York.

Lights come up on two rows of seats, arranged as on a bus. DANAE, JENNY, JAKE and TOMMY are in the seats. Actors sway to suggest the motion of a bus.

Danae: So first day of school, right? I think we just got sent a message.

Jake: Right. "Toto, I have a feeling we're not in third grade any more."

Jenny: Right, but 25 math problems *and* "How I spent my summer vacation?" The first day? Get ready for a year of no television, guys.

Danae, Jake, and Tommy: *(together, in mock horror)* No television!

Danae: Seriously, what if we get homework like this every night? How are we ever going to find time for, like, scouts and soccer practice and band practice? Not to mention television.

Tommy: *(sourly)* What band practice?

Danae: Well, you know, fourth grade, we can take instrumental music. You go to the music room and choose your instrument, and—Hey, what's the matter?

Jenny: That's right, you were away all last month. You didn't hear.

Tommy: The school board canceled instrumental music for fourth grade. It's only for fifth graders now.

Danae: *(astonished)* What!?

Jenny: There's not enough money. The school board had to get rid of some things. So they cut out band and orchestra for fourth graders.

Danae: But that's unfair!

Jake: Maybe, but my dad says you can't fight city hall. Sorry, Danae. *(gets up)* This is my stop. See you guys.

Tommy and Jenny: *(together, as Jake exits)* See you.

Spotlight centers on Danae. Another spotlight highlights the Narrator, standing at the edge of the stage with his arms folded.

Danae: That's unfair!

1 Which character in this scene has a monologue?

A Narrator

B Danae

C Jenny

D Jake

2 Who plays the part of Mr. Hallstrom in this play?

A Tommy Wu

B a music teacher

C Rob Archer

D Tarik Farshad

3 What does this stage direction from the play tell a reader?

Actors sway to suggest the motion of a bus.

A what the scenery looks like

B the expression on the actors' faces

C how the actors in the scene speak

D how the actors in the scene move

4 Which of these is part of the scenery in this play?

A an Uncle Sam costume

B a catcher's mask

C two rows of bus seats

D a single spotlight

5 What is the narrator's role in this play? How do the dialogue and stage directions suggest this role?

_____

_____

_____

_____

_____

_____

6 On a separate sheet of paper, write a scene for a play. Be sure it includes stage directions and dialogue.

In the last few lessons, you've been reading stories, poems, and plays. These are examples of **literature.** Some of the things you've had to pay attention to were the same as when you read for information. You look for the main idea. You note reasons why things happen. You connect what you're reading to what you know. You make inferences and draw conclusions about what the author means.

In literary texts, though, there are some other things to notice. The setting—where and when a story takes place—is important. Characters are important, too. You need to note details about what they are like and why they act the way they do. You have to understand the conflicts they face and the problems they must solve. A story is structured in a different way than a nonfiction article. The author presents information differently. Words don't always mean exactly what you think they mean. There may be a theme that teaches a lesson.

It's important to remember these differences when you write about literature—stories, poems, and plays. Think about how writing a book report is different from writing a social studies report. Think of how writing about a poem is different from writing about a science article. You put more of your personal thoughts and feelings into your writing when you write about literature.

On a test, you may be asked to answer questions about literary texts with a sentence, a paragraph, or an essay. Just as with nonfiction, you need to write in clear sentences and well-organized paragraphs. It helps to use graphic organizers to plan your writing. For longer answers, it's important to follow the writing process. But it's also important to pay attention to setting, characters, structure, and theme.

On some tests, you'll be asked to listen to a story and then write about it. Whether you're listening or reading, keep your mind busy:

- **Think about who the characters are and what they are like.** Think about how they relate to one another and why they do the things they do.

- **Think about the setting of the story.** Where and when does it take place? How does the setting help create the feeling of the story?

- **Think about the structure of the story.** Pay attention to the sequence of events. Note the events that set off the beginning, the middle, and the end.

- **Think about the problems in the story.** Who solves them? How are they solved?

- **Think about the theme of the story.** What lesson does it teach?

- **Take notes and use graphic organizers.** A web, for example, can help you understand a character. A timeline can help you see the sequence of events.

Guided Practice

Read a fable taken from one of the oldest collections of stories in English. Answer the questions that follow.

Chanticleer and the Fox

adapted from *The Canterbury Tales,* by Geoffrey Chaucer

There was a poor widow who lived with her two daughters in a cottage near the woods. She owned a few pigs and cows and a sheep named Molly. But the pride of her little farm was the rooster, Chanticleer. He was the finest singer in the country. His cock-a-doodle-do was the envy of the church choir. You could set the town clock by his crowing. And was he beautiful! His comb was bright red. It stood as straight as the highest tower in a castle. His bill was black and shiny. His legs were blue, and his feathers shone like gold.

He had seven hens as his wives. They were all colored just like him. His favorite was called Pertelote. She was friendly, polite, and kind. She had stolen Chanticleer's heart when he was barely out of the egg. To hear them sing together made everybody happy.

Early one morning, Pertelote saw Chanticleer going about as if with a heavy heart. "Dear husband," she said, "what is troubling you?"

"Please don't be frightened," Chanticleer replied. "I have just had the most horrible dream. I dreamed there was an animal, like a dog, that wanted to eat me. It was a yellow-red color, but its ears and tail were tipped with black. It had a small nose, and its eyes glowed red."

"Shame on you!" Pertelote replied. "I did not think I had married a coward! Don't you know that dreams are nothing? Wise men tell us to pay no attention to dreams!"

"But other wise men say just the opposite," said Chanticleer. "Well, I must put it out of my mind. It's almost dawn, and I must crow. And I must say, when I see your lovely face, I fear nothing."

All that morning Chanticleer flew around the yard and sang happily. He was no more afraid than a king in his castle. Pertelote and the other hens lay contented in the sand.

Now, it happened that a fox lived in the nearby woods. He had been watching Chanticleer and his hens greedily for three years. That night, he had broken into their yard. He hid in the garden, waiting for his chance to fall upon Chanticleer.

Suddenly, Chanticleer saw the fox. He cried out with fear. But the fox said, "Dear sir, do not be afraid! I've only come to hear you sing. You have the voice of an angel! I knew your father, you see. He was once in my house, to my great pleasure. But you—you are even a finer singer than he was! When he sang, he would close his eyes and stretch out his neck. Can you do that?"

Now, Chanticleer was so flattered that he forgot to be afraid. He closed his eyes, stretched out his neck, and crowed. At once the fox seized him by the neck and began dragging him toward the wood.

The hens began to scream. The noise alerted the widow and her daughters. They came running out. "Help! A fox!" they cried. They ran after the fox with sticks. The dogs ran after him. The cows and pigs ran after him. The neighbors came running blowing horns and shouting.

Now, listen and hear how luck can make fools of our enemies!

"Listen to them!" said Chanticleer. "How useless is all their noise! If I were you, I'd turn right now and taunt them. I'd say, 'Turn back, you fools! The rooster is my lunch!'"

The fox turned around to do just that. But as soon as he opened his mouth, Chanticleer broke free and flew high into a tree.

"O, Chanticleer!" said the fox. "I see I scared you. I was only joking. Come down and sing for me, please."

"No," said Chanticleer. "I'll not let flattery fool me twice! God will help no creature who closes his eyes when he should see!"

"No," said the fox with regret. "And bad luck, too, to the one who speaks when he should keep his mouth shut!"

What lesson does this story teach us? Use information from the story to support your answer.

Both of the main characters learn a lesson in this story. For the fox, the lesson was "Don't talk when you should keep your mouth shut." But the theme of the story is the lesson Chanticleer learns: "Listening to flattery can get you into serious trouble!" Here is a sample answer:

Chanticleer shows us the lesson of the story at the end. He says, "I'll not let flattery fool me twice! God will help no creature who closes his eyes when he should see!" He actually did close his eyes when the fox asked him to. But he really means that he was "blind" to flattery. He has a good reason to be afraid of the fox. But his fear goes away when the fox praises his singing. Luckily, he is smarter than the fox. He lives—and learns to beware of flattery!

Explain what these quotations from the story mean.

Quotation	Meaning
You could set the town clock by his crowing.	The first paragraph gives you facts and details about Chanticleer. What does this detail mean? How is a rooster like a clock? Clocks keep time, and so does a rooster by his crowing. A good answer would be: Chanticleer always crowed at exactly the right time. You could rely on him to know when it was morning.
"I knew your father, you see. He was once in my house, to my great pleasure."	What is the fox thinking of when he says this line? He means something different from what he says. Chanticleer is supposed to think that it pleased the fox to listen to his father's singing. You can infer: The fox means that his great pleasure came from eating Chanticleer's father!

You might find a question like this on a reading test. Or, you might find one that asks you to use a graphic organizer to list events of a story in order, or to organize information about a character.

Explain how this story rises, falls, and changes direction. Use examples from the story in your answer.

In your answer, be sure to explain

- what information the author gives you before you know what the story will be about
- what event helps you predict what the story will be about
- how and why Chanticleer's luck changes a few times
- what happens at the climax of the story

Read the question again carefully. It's a question about story structure. You're being asked to describe what happens in the beginning, middle, and end of the story. So the first step of prewriting should be organizing the important events of the story in a timeline like this:

Setting of the story. Character information about Chanticleer and Pertelote.

↓

Chanticleer's dream begins the middle part of the story.

↓

The fox appears. Flattery makes Chanticleer forget his fear. The fox grabs him.

↓

The people and animals chase after the fox. Chanticleer tricks the fox.

↓

Climax of the story: The fox falls for Chanticleer's trick, and Chanticleer escapes.

↓

End: Both Chanticleer and the fox have learned lessons.

The next page shows a final answer for this question. Notice how this essay is organized into paragraphs that answer each of the points of the question.

A lot happens in this short tale. It begins as a story about a happy rooster and hens. Then we get a hint of danger, but it's "only a dream." Then danger really appears. The main character is tricked, and it looks like he's had it, but he manages to escape. Will the fox trick him again? Not this time! He's learned his lesson.

The title of the story gives a hint about what the conflict will be. Everyone knows that foxes eat chickens! The beginning of the story describes the setting and the characters of Chanticleer and Pertelote. It seems like he leads a perfect, happy life. He's good looking and a fine singer. He probably knows it, too. These facts about him help us understand how the fox is able to trick him later.

Chanticleer's dream starts the middle of the story. We know from the title that there will be a fox, and a fox is what he describes. So we can predict what the conflict of the story will be before Chanticleer does. His dream has him worried, but Pertelote convinces him that his worry is foolish and cowardly. When the fox really appears, all it takes to lose his fear is for the fox to praise his singing! He shuts his eyes to danger, and just like that his luck changes from good to bad.

When the fox begins to drag Chanticleer away, everyone on the farm chases after him and makes noise. That's what gives Chanticleer the idea that saves his life. The fox opens his mouth to taunt the chasers, and at that point Chanticleer's luck changes again. The climax of the story comes when he flies away, out of the fox's reach.

But wait! The story's not over! The fox tries to fool Chanticleer a second time. There's a moment of suspense as we wonder whether Chanticleer will be tricked again. But he's learned his lesson, and so has the fox.

Test Yourself

In Lesson 13, you read part of a story about a girl who solves the problem of how to get a cat out of a tree. Now read another story about children who must solve problems. Answer the questions that follow.

Wet

by Karen Stamfil

It rained and rained. Jackson could not remember such a wet day. Of course he was only nine and couldn't remember as much as his sister Clarisse. She'd probably say it was nothing.

Running the half block from the school-bus stop left him soaked to the skin. As he dashed around the corner toward home, he saw that water filled the gutter all the way up the block. It sloshed over the curb and onto the sidewalk. The corner of Fourth and Harkness was a lake. Jackson watched a car skid through the enormous puddle. He'd have to go the long way around or he'd get even wetter.

At the corner, Jackson saw what was causing the flood. The drain was clogged with leaves and plastic bags. They made a kind of dam. Jackson looked carefully for cars. Then he reached in and pulled away the mess. It was gross, but it was satisfying to hear the water gurgling down the drain. And Clarisse thinks I can't do anything, he thought.

She was on the phone when he came in. He could tell she was talking to Mom. "But what are we supposed to *do?*" she said. When she saw him, she frowned and pointed to the bathroom. "Of *course* I can handle it…. He just came in. Looks like he's been playing in the rain…. Of *course*, mom! I'm in seventh grade now, remember?"

Jackson went into the bathroom. He washed his hands thoroughly. It was much too early for a bath, but he put on dry clothes. By the time he came out of his room, Clarisse was off the phone and busy with her homework. "Mom's going to be late getting home," she said, not looking up. "There's a mudslide blocking the highway. She has to take some roundabout way."

"What are we going to do about supper? Can we order pizza?"

"No, I'll cook."

"You?" Jackson said doubtfully.

"Sure," said Clarisse. "I'll make spaghetti. And you can clean up after. Mom said to tell you to get busy with your homework."

"I *will*, Clarisse." He glanced out the window. Water was flowing freely down the street now, and the big puddle was gone. "Can you believe all this rain? I bet it sets some kind of a record!"

"This?" Clarisse said. "This is nothing. When I was little, there was one day it rained so much it came up over the sidewalk and into the basement. Was that ever a mess!"

He wanted to tell her about the drain, but the moment had passed. She was bent over her homework, holding the eraser end of her pencil to her lower lip. Jackson knew better than to interrupt her thinking.

It was hard to concentrate on fractions. The rain was still pouring down, sweeping along the street in sheets. After a while he heard his sister get up and go into the kitchen. He heard her banging pots and pans and grunting. He was getting hungry. She would make good spaghetti, he thought. Spaghetti looked easy. But there would be a lot of sticky red sauce to clean up.

Suddenly it went dark. Just like that. Jackson heard a shriek from Clarisse. "Are you okay?" Jackson called.

"Of *course* I'm okay," Clarisse said in an irritated voice. "There's just no light!"

"The storm must have knocked out electric power," Jackson said.

"Yeah, no kidding," his sister said. "Looks like it's out all over the neighborhood. How am I supposed to—*ouch!*—cook in the dark?"

"We can light candles," Jackson said. He groped his way into the kitchen. It wasn't hard to do because he knew the house so well. "I can hold the flashlight for you."

Unit 3 Reading and Writing with Literature 159

"Already thought of that," Clarisse said. She was opening the drawer where Mom kept things like string and scissors. He could see her by the blue-yellow light of the stove's gas burner. She pulled out something round and solid. "Right, no batteries," she said, clicking the switch on and off. "No candles either. Mom has them both on the shopping list."

Jackson thought hard. He knew there had to be something they could do. He wanted very much to be the one who thought of it. And he did.

He felt his way to his room. He groped in his closet until he found his remote-controlled car. On his dresser was a clock radio. He usually kept it plugged in, but it ran on batteries, too. He hoped the ones in there were still good.

"Some of these ought to work," Jackson said, returning to the kitchen. He poured the batteries into Clarisse's hands. "Better hurry. You know how you hate mushy spaghetti."

There was plenty left over for Mom when she got home. "What a day!" she said, putting away her umbrella. "I can't remember the last time it rained like this!"

"This?" said Jackson, grinning at his sister. "This is nothing!"

1 Clarisse and Jackson have to solve three problems before their mother gets home. What are these problems, and how do they solve them?

The first problem:	Solution:
The second problem:	Solution:
The third problem:	Solution:

2 Why did Jackson "want very much" to come up with a solution to the battery problem? Use examples from the story to explain your answer.

_____

_____

_____

_____

_____

_____

3
> Write a story about solving a problem. Describe what you were doing, what the problem was, and how you solved it.
>
> In your story, be sure to include
>
> • a title for your story
>
> • a clear beginning, middle, and end to your story
>
> • specific details to make your story interesting

Use the space below for prewriting. Write a title for your story. Then write your draft on the next page. Revise, edit, and proofread your story. Check your writing for correct spelling, grammar, capitalization, and punctuation. Lastly, write your final answer on a separate sheet of paper.

Use the space below to write your draft.

Unit 3 Reading and Writing with Literature

Unit 4: Reading and Writing for Critical Analysis

What does "critical analysis" mean? It means that you have to think about what you read and ask yourself some questions. What was the author's purpose for writing this? Is someone trying to persuade me to buy something or to think in a certain way? Is this information true and correct? What is the source? Is it a fact that can be proven, or someone's opinion? What is the author's point of view?

Lessons 21–25 help you learn to think about or analyze what you read and write.

21 Author's Purpose   It's important to examine the point of view of an author and find the author's purpose or reason for writing what you're reading.

22 Fact and Opinion   In this lesson you will learn to tell the difference between the facts and opinions in reading selections.

23 Analyzing Ideas   Many times, your own ideas and experiences help you understand another person's thoughts or feelings when you're reading. This lesson will help you find themes so that you can better understand the message the writer is trying to get across.

24 Making Judgments   You will learn how to "check out the facts" in this lesson— and why it's important to find out if information is true and accurate.

25 Writing to Analyze   This lesson shows you how to write from different points of view. Now that you've learned to analyze facts, details, and opinions, you will write a response that persuades or shows what you know.

Author's Purpose

Authors have different reasons for writing. When you read, think about *why* the author is writing. You can find clues in the way the author presents information, the point of view, and the details the author chooses to include.

A poster or ad that contains many opinions or that tries to get you to do something is usually meant to **persuade.**

Something with a lot of details, such as a travel book, is usually meant to **describe.**

A passage full of facts or directions is usually meant to **explain** or **instruct.**

A story or a poem is usually meant to **entertain** or **amuse.**

Guided Practice

Read these two selections and answer the questions that follow.

Selection 1

"One of the year's 10 best"
—KIDS' BOOK WORLD

No Graves in Egypt
by Paula Thomas

Hub Bailes gets along by minding his own business. Where can he turn for help when he is mistaken for a runaway slave?

"Page-turning excitement"
—history_is_fun.org

CL-2507   **Special club price $5.95**

Selection 2

No Graves in Egypt, by Paula Thomas. New York: Goodspeed Books, 176 pp.

No Graves in Egypt has nothing to do with tombs or mummies. It's Paula Thomas's new novel set in America's past. Like all her historical fiction, it is full of page-turning excitement. But those who like real history with their fiction may be disappointed.

No Graves in Egypt is the story of Hub Bailes. He is an African American boy in Syracuse, New York. The year is 1855. In the South, African Americans were enslaved. Hub was born free. He has been to school. He works on a canal boat, traveling from one end of the state to the other.

Into his life comes the Powell family. They have escaped from slavery in Virginia. They are being hunted by "slave catchers" Drury and Cates. Sojourner Truth (a real person) wants Hub to help the Powells get to Canada. To Hub, their troubles are not his business. He does not want to risk going to jail. Then Hub himself is mistaken for a runaway slave. Before the action ends, he comes to realize that freedom is everyone's business.

Young readers will identify with Hub and his conflicts. Other characters are not so true to life. Sojourner Truth speaks like a modern college-educated woman. (In real life, she could not read or write.) Cates and Drury are cardboard bad guys. Among the Powell family, only 10-year-old Jane stands out as an individual. Still, Paula Thomas tells a good story. Her fans should enjoy reading *No Graves in Egypt.*

In Selection 1, the author's purpose is to

   A   explain the plot of *No Graves in Egypt*

   B   get people to buy *No Graves in Egypt*

   C   describe the setting of *No Graves in Egypt*

   D   tell an entertaining story set in the past

> You probably recognized this selection as an advertisement. Like all advertising, its purpose is to persuade. It includes details that might make you want to buy the book. Choice B is the correct answer.

Which of these details **best** supports the author's purpose?

   A   One of the year's 10 best

   B   by Paula Thomas

   C   Hub Bailes gets along by minding his own business.

   D   history_is_fun.org

> The selection contains positive comments, an idea of the plot, and "special club price" information. These details support the purpose of selling the book. The author's name might persuade people who like her books, but it is not part of the "sales pitch." Choice A is the answer.

In Selection 2, the author's purpose is to

   A   give an entertaining summary of the plot

   B   persuade people not to buy the book

   C   explain the historical details that are in the book

   D   give a description and an opinion of the book

> You probably recognized this selection as a book review. It contains details about the plot, characters, and setting. It includes both positive and negative opinions. You might or might not want to buy the book after reading the selection. Choice D is correct.

Use a separate sheet of paper to answer this question. Suppose the author of Selection 2 had wanted to write an exciting summary of the plot of *No Graves in Egypt*. What other kinds of details would she have included? What is one detail in the selection that she would **not** have included?

Now read this selection and answer the questions that follow.

A Pig's Life
A folktale from India

A Hindu teacher had a dream. Now, the Hindu people believe that when a person dies, his spirit is reborn to another life. In his dream, the teacher saw what his next life would be. The next day he saw his favorite student. He asked him, "Will you grant me a favor in return for all I have given you?"

"Yes, certainly," said the student. "I will do whatever you ask me to do."

"Then listen," said the teacher. "I know I am going to die soon. I have learned that I will be reborn as a pig! Can you imagine anything more terrible?"

"Oh, no, Master!" said the student. "Surely you must be mistaken!"

"I wish I were," said the teacher miserably. "Do you see that sow eating garbage over there? I will be reborn as the fourth piglet of her next litter. You'll know me by a mark on my forehead. When she has her litter, find the fourth piglet with the mark on its forehead. Kill it with your knife. That way I will be released from a pig's life. Perhaps I'll have better luck in my next life."

The student was sad to hear this, but he promised to do what the teacher asked. Sure enough, soon afterward the teacher did die. And the sow did have a litter of piglets. And indeed, the fourth one had a mark on its forehead.

So one day, the student sharpened his knife. But just as he was about to cut the little pig's throat, it screamed, "Stop! Don't kill me!"

Before the student could recover from his surprise, the piglet went on. "Don't kill me," it repeated. "I want to live a pig's life. Before, when I asked you to kill me, I had no idea about what it would be like. It's great to be a pig! Now, let me go!"

What **best** describes the main purpose of this passage?

    A   to persuade people not to kill animals

    B   to explain the beliefs of Hindu people

    C   to teach a lesson in an amusing way

    D   to describe what a pig's life is like

> You've read enough folktales to understand their purpose: to tell an entertaining story. But it's usually more than just a story. There's a message or "moral" about the way we humans behave. That's why we can appreciate such tales no matter what culture they come from. Choice C is the correct answer.

Which of these details does **not** support the author's purpose?

    A   the teacher and student being friends

    B   the teacher's dream about being reborn as a pig

    C   the student knowing which piglet had been his teacher

    D   the piglet speaking just as the student is about to kill him

> Which details are important either to the story or to its lesson? The pig is an animal that few cultures respect. So the teacher's feeling that it would better to be dead than to live "a pig's life" is an important detail. If the student was going to kill an ordinary pig, or if the piglet hadn't spoken, there would be no story. But it's not the author's purpose to show that the teacher and student are friends. Choice A is correct.

The author uses a third-person point of view. He lets you know some of the thoughts of both the teacher and the student. How would the story be different if it had a first-person point of view?

_____

_____

_____

_____

_____

_____

Test Yourself

Now read this selection and answer the questions that follow.

I have a new name and a new home. I have a new life, really. Joyce used to call me Buttermilk. That was such a very long time ago! But I've thought of myself as Buttermilk ever since. All those years shut away in the dark, I used to remind myself, "Buttermilk. Your name is Buttermilk." Now that I'm Molly, I have to get used to it.

I was called Buttermilk because I'm a light tan color. Not light enough to be white, and not dark enough to be brown. But my mane is a dark chocolate brown. So is my tail. And I have four brown socks, one above each hoof. My ears are far apart. Joyce used to slide her finger between them. She said that meant I had a lot of brain space. But it's not polite to brag about how smart you are, even if it's true.

Joyce played with me for hours. There were nine of us most of the time. There was Champion, Big Red, Dusty, and Queen of the Wind. There was Tornado too, but the less said about him, the better. (It's fine to buck and snort, but there are limits!) We all thought we were Joyce's favorite. And I guess we all were, at one time. Sometimes Joyce's friends would come and bring their favorites, and we'd have a grand time riding the range.

Then there came a time when Joyce didn't play with us much any more. Then she stopped playing with us at all. For a long time we sat on a shelf in her room. We got dusty. (Even Dusty got dusty. That was a big joke for a while.) Then we kind of got moved from place to place. At last we were shut away in the dark place. We got on as best we could with each other's company. After a while the others stopped missing Joyce so much. But I never did.

Then suddenly it was light again. A woman came and took us out of our box. Big Red said she was a stranger, but she kind of reminded me of Joyce. Anyway, she gave us all a bath. She held me up and smiled and kissed me like Joyce used to. Then she set us outdoors on a blanket. We were with a lot of old toys and books and things I remembered from Joyce's room. And that's when Samantha and her dad came and took me away.

Like I said, Samantha calls me Molly. I think we're going to get along okay. I miss the others. But the truth is, they had gotten a little too familiar all those years in the dark place. I think change is good.

1 The author's purpose in this selection is to

    A describe a woman's favorite childhood toy

    B relate facts and details about toys of earlier days

    C tell an amusing story about a toy horse

    D get readers interested in books about horses

2 Which of these is a clue that **best** suggests the author's purpose?

    A the names of the horses in paragraph 3

    B a horse that bucks and snorts

    C details of the selection's setting

    D the selection's point of view

3 The author's main purpose in the second paragraph is to

    A explain how Buttermilk got her name

    B give readers a mental picture of Buttermilk

    C make readers feel a certain way about Buttermilk

    D give readers facts and details about horses

4 Suppose the author were to add more details to paragraph 3.
What kind of details would best fit there?

_____

_____

_____

_____

_____

_____

5 Use a separate sheet of paper. Write an advertisement to
persuade people that they should buy horse models. Use the
information in this selection about toy horses.

Fact and Opinion

When you read nonfiction, you are reading facts—mostly. Some of the statements you read may be the author's opinions. As you read, you need to figure out which statements are opinions and which are facts. A fact is a statement that can be proven by seeing it or by looking it up. It is true for everyone. An opinion is a statement of what the author thinks or feels. It is true only for some people.

These words can be clues that the author is expressing an opinion:

feel   nobody
believe   never   seem
worst   think   always
best   all

Guided Practice

Read a student's book report. Answer the questions that follow.

The Laurel Crown
by Frank Maltesi

The Laurel Crown takes place during the Olympic Games. These are not the modern Olympics that are on TV. These are the original Olympics of ancient Greece. Author Frank Maltesi tells an exciting sports story. But readers also learn some interesting facts about history.

It is the year 436 BC. Timaeus is a 20-year-old runner from the city of Athens. He has come to Olympia to compete in the games. His chief rival is Gorgias of Sparta. Most of the action is the drama leading up to their race. Gorgias will stop at nothing to win the laurel crown. (That's

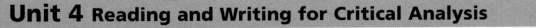

Unit 4 Reading and Writing for Critical Analysis　　**171**

a prize made of leaves that goes to the winner.) Timaeus also does things that we would call cheating. It seems that the Greek Olympics were like pro sports today. Winning was the only thing that mattered. A winner's home city would give him gold. He might be excused from paying taxes for the rest of his life. Second place counted for nothing.

There is more going on in *The Laurel Crown* than sports, though. The book really involves you in history. War is brewing between Athens and Sparta. You learn why these two cities don't like each other. You learn that the Olympics started as a religious festival. (Some of the religious customs, like sacrificing 100 bulls to the god Zeus, were pretty gross.) You find out what words like *stadium* and *gymnasium* originally meant. You learn how hard it was to be a slave in that culture, or a woman. You really feel that you are at the ancient Olympics with all their sights, sounds, and smells.

But mostly it is a sports story. Anyone who enjoys fiction about sports will like *The Laurel Crown.* The book is easy to read. The action on the training grounds and on the track never lets up. The characters are realistic, even though they lived long ago. Timaeus is someone you'd want on your team. Gorgias is someone you'd love to beat. You'll meet a blind musician with a mysterious past and a funny food seller who may be doing some not-so-funny things to the food. The ending will surprise you, yet it is completely believable. As historical fiction and as a sports story, *The Laurel Crown* wins a gold medal.

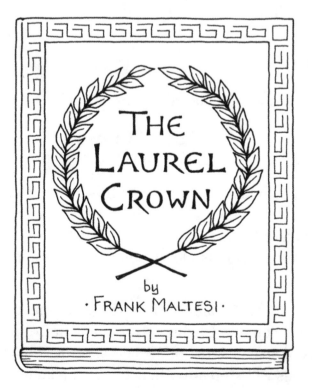

Which of these statements in the first paragraph is an opinion?

A *The Laurel Crown* takes place during the Olympic Games.

B These are not the modern Olympics that are on TV.

C These are the original Olympics of ancient Greece.

D Author Frank Maltesi tells an exciting sports story.

> The first three answer choices are all statements you could prove by reading the book. But is it a fact that the story is exciting? That's an opinion of the student who wrote the book report. Someone else might not think it's so exciting. Choice D is the correct answer.

Which of these statements is a fact about *The Laurel Crown?*

A Readers learn some interesting facts about history.

B The book takes place in the year 436 BC.

C The main character, Timaeus, is a cheat.

D The Greek Olympics were like pro sports today.

> Check each sentence to decide whether it can be proved. In choice A, "interesting" is an opinion word. The writer doesn't say that Timaeus cheats. It just says that *we* would call it cheating. It's also the writer's opinion that the Greek Olympics were like pro sports today. "Like" in what way? The one choice you could prove is the date of the events in the book. Choice B is the answer.

Which of these is the reviewer's opinion about ancient Greece?

A An Olympic winner's home city might give him gold.

B The Greek Olympics started as a religious festival.

C Some of the religious customs were pretty gross.

D One custom was to sacrifice 100 bulls to the god Zeus.

> You could prove some of these statements by reading nonfiction about ancient Greece. You'd find that an Olympic winner often was awarded money by his city. The Olympics were a religious festival. But is it a fact that the customs were "gross"? That's a "feeling word" used by the reviewer—an opinion. Choice C is correct.

Which of these statements about the book is a fact?

A The book is easy to read.

B The action never lets up.

C You really feel that you are at the ancient Olympics.

D You learn the original meanings of *gymnasium* and *stadium*.

> Which statement can be proven? The book may have been "easy" for the reviewer to read, but maybe not for other people. In choice B, "never" is an opinion word. The writer may "really feel" that the book places him at the ancient Olympics, but he can't know what anyone else would feel. Reading the book could show you if it says what *gymnasium* and *stadium* originally meant, and you can check in a reference book to be sure. Choice D is the only fact, and the answer you want.

How would you summarize the reviewer's opinion of the book? Explain your answer with examples from the selection.

_____

_____

_____

_____

_____

_____

_____

Test Yourself

Read an article about an unusual school project. Answer the questions that follow.

At Lynnwood Elementary School in Guilderland, New York, the fourth grade is learning about Native American life. That's not surprising. Fourth-graders across America study the Native American cultures of their state. But Lynnwood students do it in a wonderful way. They build an Iroquois village next to their school.

"It was very exciting," says one student. "I had never built anything like that before. It made me feel like I really was an Iroquois."

The Iroquois village project was the idea of three Lynnwood teachers. It has been going on since 1999. Every fall, fourth graders bring history to life. They spend weeks studying the Iroquois in class. They read legends and learn about Iroquois culture. They take a field trip to Albany to study the Iroquois longhouse at the New York State Museum. Each class chooses a "chief" in the traditional Iroquois way. (That is, the "chief" is a boy, but it's the girls who choose him.)

Then the building of the village begins. Teachers and parents help the students. They use materials the Iroquois would have used 400 years ago. They find them in the woods near the school.

"It's such an exciting way to learn history," one parent comments. "It gives the kids an understanding they couldn't get any other way. They learn what life was like several hundred years ago."

At the center of the village is an Iroquois longhouse. It is eight feet high. Nearby are racks for drying fish and hides. There are fire circles and a vegetable garden. Students role-play Iroquois clan members. For a week they guide visitors on tours of the village. They display traditional Iroquois craftwork they have made in class. "We learned how to make things by hand that we actually make with machines today," one student says proudly.

an Iroquois longhouse

All Lynnwood fourth graders look forward to the project every year. It is always a success. Students, teachers, and parents alike are excited about it. Children learn the value of working as a team. It is a wonderful way for people in the community to get to know each other.

On the last day, the "Iroquois" have a closing ceremony. It is interrupted by the arrival of "European" traders, played by teachers, the school secretary, and the principal. They offer to trade goods in exchange for the Native Americans' land. The students discuss whether the trade is a good idea.

Then the village is taken apart. By the end of the day, it is completely gone. The site is ready for next year's fourth graders.

1 Which of these statements is an opinion?

    A Fourth graders across America study Native American life.

    B Lynnwood students do it in a wonderful way.

    C They build an Iroquois village next to their school.

    D The school is in Guilderland, New York.

2 Which of these statements about the Iroquois village is a fact?

    A It is an exciting way to learn history.

    B It gives kids an understanding they couldn't get any other way.

    C Parents and teachers work together with students.

    D All Lynnwood fourth graders look forward to the project.

3 Which of these statements is **not** a fact?

    A At the center of the students' village is an Iroquois longhouse.

    B For a week students guide visitors on tours of the village.

    C They make things by hand to display in the village.

    D Children learn the value of working as a team.

4 Identify sentences in the article that are the opinions of three different people. Write the sentences below. Tell whose opinion each of them is.

_____

_____

_____

_____

_____

5 On a separate sheet of paper, write a paragraph about a special project you have done in school. Make sure it includes at least two sentences that are facts and two sentences that are your opinions.

Unit 4 Reading and Writing for Critical Analysis

Analyzing Ideas

Standard 3.R.1.b, e; 3.R.2, 3; 3.R.7.a; 3.W.8, 9

You understand and enjoy reading more when what you read relates to your own knowledge and experience. What you know helps you understand a character's feelings. It gives you clues about whether something is realistic or not realistic, true or false. It helps you recognize themes that pop up again and again in fiction, nonfiction, and even in poetry.

Unit 4 Reading and Writing for Critical Analysis

Guided Practice

Read these two poems and answer the questions that follow.

Maple Leaves

by Shiko (1664–1731)

They make us jealous,
Becoming so beautiful—
Red leaves in fall

The Last Leaf

by Marcia Roche-Tombée

The
last leaf
leaves the
baby birch
one December
day. Its friends all
have flown, the wind
has blown them all away.
Still one remained through
October rains, November winds,
The first December fall of snow
that bent the branches low,
bone-bare, except for one
leaf, brown and thin.
But now it's gone
and winter
can
be
gi
n.

The theme of "Maple Leaves" is

A wanting something you can't have   **C** someone plain wanting to be beautiful

B admiring the beauty of nature   **D** feelings that the color red suggests

> This poem mentions jealousy, but it isn't about jealousy. It's about how we feel when the leaves take on their fall colors. We think, "How beautiful!" You've probably had that feeling yourself. Also, you may have recognized this poem as a haiku, and haiku are usually about nature. Choice B is the correct answer.

"The Last Leaf" suggests a feeling of

A joyful anticipation of winter holidays

B grumbling about bad weather

C the impatience of waiting for snow

D sadness at the dying of the year

> Winter can bring on many different feelings. It's a time of holidays and fun in the snow. But "The Last Leaf" is full of images of sadness. The leaf's friends have all gone away, leaving it alone. The branches are compared to bones. The poet is expressing sadness about the passing of life. You probably know that feeling too, and that choice D is correct.

From the two poems, one idea that is **not** realistic is

A a person wanting to be like something in nature

B leaves turning red in fall

C a leaf remaining on a tree after an autumn storm

D leaves having friends

> You know that poems can sometimes use language to create pictures in ways that are not quite real. Think of the ideas in these two poems. You know that leaves do turn red, and that a leaf sometimes can remain on a tree long after the others have fallen. You also know that people may daydream about being as beautiful as a butterfly or as strong as a lion. But leaves don't really have friends. Choice D is the correct answer.

Unit 4 Reading and Writing for Critical Analysis   **179**

Both these poems are about

A how we feel about trees

C how quickly time passes

B changing seasons

D days when we feel lonely

> These two poems suggest very different feelings. But both sets of feelings come from the same experience—watching the seasons change. That's an experience we've all had. Choice B is correct.

The speaker in "The Last Leaf" suggests that winter begins when the last leaf is off the trees. Explain why you agree or disagree.

_____

_____

_____

_____

_____

_____

Test Yourself

Now read this selection and answer the questions that follow.

Meet a Firefighter

Teresa Johnson works as a firefighter for the United States Forest Service. Her team travels all over the western states putting out forest fires. In this interview she talks about her work and how she feels about it.

Interviewer: You're from Brooklyn. Why are you fighting fires way out West instead of in New York City?

Teresa: I'm still a big-city girl. But I've always loved being where I can be surrounded by trees, whether it's Prospect Park or Yellowstone National Park. In high school I read *Young Men and Fire* by Norman McLean. It's a true story about a forest fire in

Montana and the people who fought it. I suppose that's when my dream started to take shape.

Interviewer: Did you go out West and sign up after you graduated?

Teresa: No, my first job was as a nurse's aide. But I took a wilderness survival course in the Adirondacks one summer. Then I was in the army for two years, and I learned to fly helicopters. All those things eventually helped me get where I am today. Realizing a dream can be a roundabout thing. You have to turn it into a goal at some point. You have to stop dreaming and start planning.

Interviewer: What was your plan?

Teresa: I walked into a Forest Service office one day and applied for a job. That was in Basalt, Colorado. I filled out a form. I listed my skills. I knew how to use a chain saw and how to give first aid. I was good at working with a team, taking orders, making quick decisions when I had to. I had to pass a fitness test. You have to be able to fight your way uphill carrying heavy equipment. And you have to be able to run. Anyway, I was back home a month later when I got a letter offering me a job! I took a training program in California. They started me out doing the basic grunt work, but I took every chance I had to learn a new skill or piece of equipment. Now I'm a qualified trainer myself.

Interviewer: What's a typical day like on your job?

Teresa: I don't know that there is such a thing as a typical day. In peak fire season, you might be out in the field for five months and on the line fighting fires three weeks straight. When you're not fighting fires, you work in prevention. You go out and measure how dry and how thick the brush is. That tells you where danger is greatest. You clear trails and roads for emergency trucks. You set small, controlled fires to prevent big ones. When you do that, you work with tree and wildlife scientists. Some days you work in an office at a computer. And some days you lead kids through the woods to teach them about fire safety.

Interviewer: What can kids do to help prevent forest fires?

Teresa: Just what Smokey Bear always says. Don't smoke. Make sure campfires are completely out. And use common sense.

1 What is the theme of Teresa Johnson's interview?

    A   Have a goal and a plan for achieving it.

    B   Anyone can make a dream come true.

    C   Someone from a city can find a career outdoors.

    D   You never know what skills may come in handy.

2 It's most likely that Teresa's two years in the army

    A   gave her experience at fighting fires

    B   helped her lose her fear of fire

    C   taught her to work with a team

    D   helped her realize her dream

3 Which of the following **best** describes how Teresa Johnson probably feels when she's on her way to fight a fire?

    A   happy, because she's getting to do what she likes

    B   frightened, because forest fires are dangerous

    C   proud, because she knows she is good at her job

    D   bored, because she may be at it for three weeks

4 What are some events that happened to Teresa Johnson that support the message she's giving to her readers?

_____

_____

_____

_____

_____

5 Use a separate sheet of paper. Imagine that someone is interviewing you 20 years from now about **your** job. Write some of the interviewer's questions and your answers.

Unit 4 Reading and Writing for Critical Analysis

Making Judgments

Standard 3.R.5, 8; 3.W.3, 5

"Don't believe everything you read." You've probably heard this warning from a parent or teacher. You can't check every fact you read. How can you tell whether what you're reading is true and accurate (or correct)? Here are some things to think about.

- **Think about the author's purpose.** Is she trying to persuade you to agree with her? Is he trying to sell you something? Is she trying to tell a good story rather than to give information? In such cases, some of the "facts" you read may not be correct.

- **Think about the source.** Can you trust that the author knows what he's talking about? Is it an expert or your Aunt Faye? Is the source a book publisher or newspaper that checks facts? Or is it just someone exercising his right of free speech?

- **Think about what you know.** Does the information go against common sense, your experience, or something else you've read? How did you learn what you know? Better check it out!

- **Think about facts and opinions.** Does the author offer a lot of opinions without backing them up with facts? Maybe you should check a second source.

Unit 4 Reading and Writing for Critical Analysis   **183**

Guided Practice

Read some selections from a newspaper. Answer the questions that follow.

Selection 1

High-Rise Hawks in New Nest

NEW YORK—Pale Male and Lola are home.

The two red-tailed hawks were building a new nest Tuesday. It is near their old nesting site on the 12th floor ledge of an apartment building. Bird experts prepared a special nest for them. Hours after they left, Pale Male and Lola were back home at Fifth Avenue and 74th Street. They were spotted taking twigs back to the nest.

The hawks have nested on the high rise since 1993. People complained that they were a health and safety hazard. Their droppings and remains of their prey sometimes fell on the sidewalk. The nest was taken down earlier this month. But there were angry protests from bird lovers. The building's owners finally agreed to let the birds return. The new nest is designed for safety.

Not everyone is pleased. "Those birds don't belong in the city," said Ms. Jean Gallo, a neighbor. "They eat people's dogs and cats, you know. They belong in the woods somewhere."

Most of the crowd outside the building, however, seemed glad to see the hawks back.

Selection 2

Dear Entertainment Editor:

Why was my favorite TV Show, "Star Patrol," canceled? And don't tell me it was because the ratings were bad. I know that's not true because all my friends watch the show. I want the real reason, please.

Terry Bell
Queens, NY

Selection 3

You won't want to miss our once-in-a-lifetime video and DVD sale! Buy one at full price, and you can take home two others of the same or lower price ABSOLUTELY FREE. Better hurry! The offer is good only through Feb. 16. And while you're here, check out our other GREAT BUYS on video and hi-fi equipment!

Sam's Video and Hi-Fi

55 West 21st Street • 1-800-555-0995 • samsvid@bpm.com

Offer applies only to specially labeled items.
No returns or exchanges on sale items.

Buy 1, Get 2 Free!
(While They Last!)

From Selection 1, which information is **most likely** true and accurate?

    A   Two hawks are nesting on a New York City high rise.

    B   They are a health and safety hazard.

    C   The new nest is designed for safety.

    D   Most people are glad to see the hawks back.

> Let's say that this article is from a good newspaper. So the basic facts are probably true and accurate. But read the article carefully. "People complained" that the birds were a health and safety hazard. What people? And who says that the new nest is designed for safety? The article doesn't tell you. In the last sentence, the word "seemed" tells you that it's the reporter's opinion. Choice A is the statement that is most likely accurate, so it is the correct answer.

Ms. Jean Gallo is quoted as saying that the hawks "eat people's dogs and cats." What source would you check to find out if this is true?

    A Ms. Gallo   **C** a scientist who studies hawks

    B the reporter who wrote the article   **D** a friend who knows a lot about birds

> Where did Ms. Gallo get this information? Maybe she just heard it from a friend of hers whose cat is missing. Nothing suggests that the reporter is an expert on birds. And your friend may know about birds, but probably not as much as the scientist. Choice C is the correct answer.

In Selection 3, which of these statements is **most** certain to be truthful?

    A It's a once-in-a lifetime sale.

    B The offer is only good through February 16.

    C Buy any movie at full price and you get two free.

    D There are other great buys on video equipment.

> You can tell that the purpose of this ad is to get people to shop at Sam's Video. And you know that businesses don't really give anything away free. You can infer that "once-in-a-lifetime" means only until the next sale. You could compare prices at other stores to check whether Sam offers "great buys." The one fact you can probably count on is that the DVD and video sale ends February 16, choice B.

You can tell that not every DVD is on sale by looking carefully at

A the illustration

C the paragraph at the right

B the words in capital letters

D the small print at the bottom

Many businesses mark up the "regular" price on an item. That makes a "sale" price seem very low. Another sales trick they use is to suggest that "more is better." You may only want one DVD, not three. Businesses also advertise a sale to get you into the store. Then they try to sell you other, more expensive items. Chances are, the DVDs and videos on sale at Sam's are not the titles people most want to buy. They're ones that the store wants to clear out. Read the small print at the bottom. Choice D is the correct answer.

In Selection 2, Terry Bell doesn't believe that his favorite TV show was canceled due to bad ratings—too few people watching. Is his statement truthful and accurate? Explain why or why not.

_____

_____

_____

_____

_____

_____

Use a separate sheet of paper to answer this question. Suppose you had to write a report on a foreign country. What would be the **most** accurate and truthful source you could use? What source would be the least accurate? Explain why.

Test Yourself

Now read another group of selections and answer the questions that follow.

Selection 1

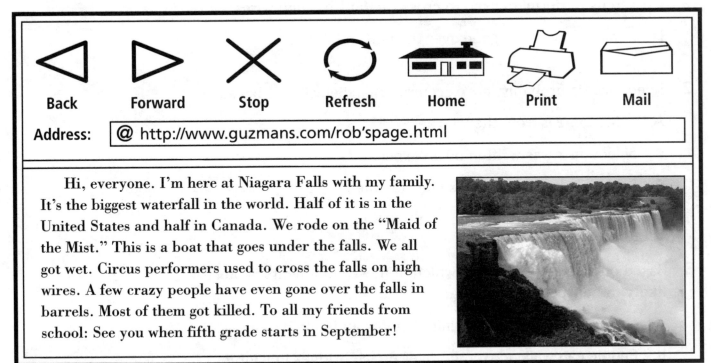

Back   Forward   Stop   Refresh   Home   Print   Mail

Address: @ http://www.guzmans.com/rob'spage.html

Hi, everyone. I'm here at Niagara Falls with my family. It's the biggest waterfall in the world. Half of it is in the United States and half in Canada. We rode on the "Maid of the Mist." This is a boat that goes under the falls. We all got wet. Circus performers used to cross the falls on high wires. A few crazy people have even gone over the falls in barrels. Most of them got killed. To all my friends from school: See you when fifth grade starts in September!

Selection 2

Niagara Falls Facts and Figures
by Megan Pratt, Ph.D., Professor of Geology, SUNY

- Location: on the Niagara River, forming the border between New York state and the Canadian province of Ontario

- Height: 176 feet (53.6 m) on U.S. side, 167 feet (50.9 m) on Canadian side

- Average flow: 750,000 gallons (2.8 million liters) per second. One-fifth of the world's fresh water flows over Niagara Falls. About three-fourths of the bank and four-fifths of the flow is on the Canadian side.

- Many of the world's waterfalls are higher than Niagara. But only Africa's Victoria Falls has a greater flow.

- Niagara Falls is more than 10,000 years old. It was formed by glaciers during the last Ice Age. The falls is slowly wearing away the underlying rock.

- An ice bridge may form across the Niagara River in winter. But only once has ice been observed to completely block the flow over the falls. This happened on March 29, 1848.

- *Maid of the Mist* boat tours run from April through October. The present *Maid of the Mist* is the 11th boat of that name. The boats have been carrying people under the falls since 1846.

- A schoolteacher was the first person ever to survive a ride over the falls in a barrel. She was 63 years old.

Selection 3

© The Continental Press, Inc.   Do not duplicate.

1 Which of these statements in Selection 1 is probably **not** true?

   A Niagara Falls is the biggest waterfall in the world.

   B The "Maid of the Mist" is a boat that goes under the falls.

   C Circus performers used to cross the falls on high wires.

   D Some people have gone over the falls in barrels.

2 Selection 2 is probably **more** accurate than Selection 1 because

   A Selection 1 is from the Internet

   B Selection 2 was written by an expert

   C Selection 1 was written as entertainment

   D Selection 2 was written more recently

3 Based on Selections 1 and 2, which of these statements is **most likely** to be true and accurate?

   A Half of the falls is in the United States and half in Canada.

   B People can walk across the river on ice bridges in winter.

   C Everyone who rides on the "Maid of the Mist" boat gets wet.

   D Niagara Falls was formed by glaciers during the Ice Age.

4 Can you trust that the information in Selection 3 is true and accurate? Explain why or why not.

_____

_____

_____

_____

_____

5 Choose an article or advertisement from today's newspaper. On a separate sheet of paper, explain what may not be true and accurate about it, and why.

Unit 4 Reading and Writing for Critical Analysis

Standard 3.W.1, 2, 3, 4, 7, 8, 9

Sometimes when you write, you are expressing your opinion and point of view. When you do that, you need to back up your opinion with facts. At other times, you might write to respond to someone else's opinion and point of view. To do that, you have to **analyze** or think about what you read. A test question may ask you to draw information from two or more sources for your answer. Then you may need to compare and contrast two different points of view.

When you write to analyze and respond to other points of view, all the rules of good writing still apply. Have a clear main idea. Plan your writing. Use strong, complete sentences and well-organized paragraphs. Make sure there are strong, clear connections between your ideas. Revise and proofread what you write. Keep your mind busy as you read and plan. Analyze and think about what you're reading and what you will write.

- **Think about the author's purpose.** It can help you recognize why she may have a particular point of view.

- **Pay attention to facts and opinions.** It might be helpful to list them separately in a graphic organizer.

- **Think about what you know.** How does it connect with the facts and opinions to help you draw conclusions?

- **Think about the source.** Consider the author's point of view. Can you trust that what he says is true and correct, or should you check another source?

- **Figure out connections.** Compare and contrast information from different sources. (A graphic organizer can help you do this.) What conclusions can you draw about the information?

SLUGS FROM SATURN

"THE SCI-FI THRILLER OF THE YEAR! DON'T MISS IT!"

PASS THE SALT! "SLUGS" IS AWFUL!!

Guided Practice

In Lesson 21, you read a story told by a toy horse. Now read an article about people who collect horse models and answer the question that follows.

Horse Dreams
by Rebecca Zeitlin

Silver rears up on his hind legs, above the other horses in their green-carpeted corral. That's the Lone Ranger's trusty steed. Tonto's pony, Scout, is nearby. But the Lone Ranger and Tonto are not here. There are no riders here, only horses. Still, anyone old enough to remember those great days of TV's yesteryear can't help matching the absent riders with their horses. That "golden palomino" is Roy Rogers' famous horse, Trigger. Buttermilk and Trigger were probably good buddies. Buttermilk was the pride of Dale Evans, "Queen of the West." Thousands of little girls were proud to own the model of Buttermilk. And long ago, I was one of those little girls.

I'm in a high school gym, at a meeting of the Washington County Horse Model Collectors' Club. Around me are tables and display cases covered with horses. There are ceramic horses, metal horses, and old hand-carved wooden horses. I see some ponies that are no bigger than the bride on a wedding cake. But most of the models are the foot-long molded plastic horses I played with as a child.

A collector in cowgirl clothes tells me that these horses were made by Breyer® Animal Creations® in New Jersey. The woman's name tag identifies her as Liz Campbell. Liz shows me the name "Breyer" on the inside of Silver's left hind leg. "Other companies make them too, but Breyer has been in the business the longest. If you're going to collect horse models, Breyers are the way to go. Most of the horses here are Breyers. The ones you played with were probably Breyers, too."

That was during the 1950s. You could hardly turn on the TV then without seeing horses. Growing up in the Bronx, I used to dream that I would someday live "out in the country," where I could own a horse. But if I couldn't have a real horse, at least I had my models. I added to the herd on birthdays and holidays and any time I could scrape up five bucks from my allowance. (That was real money for a kid then!) I'd get together with my friends Susie and Diane, who had their own collections. We'd make up stories and plays about the horses. We'd race them. I even knitted little saddle blankets for them.

I'd never heard of the Breyer name back then. But I'm hearing it a lot at the Collectors' Club. "They made their first model horse in 1950," Liz Campbell explains. "It was ordered by a clock company to go on one of their clocks. When the company didn't pay them, Breyer kept the mold. They sold the models to stores, and they just kept selling."

There haven't been westerns on TV for years, so I was surprised to learn that kids today still play with horse models. A flock of little girls, and a few boys too, are admiring the models on display. They still read the same books about horses we did 50 years ago. Walter Farley's *Black Stallion* series and Marguerite Henry's *Misty of Chincoteague* are still favorites. There's a Breyer model for almost every horse made famous in fiction. There are models of different breeds and of famous racehorses, too. Some people collect only one particular breed or color. And there are the famous old TV horses from my childhood. Judging by the prices, I never should have let my mother give them away. New Breyers, such as Hidalgo, from the recent movie, start at around $25. Some of the hard-to-find older models go for hundreds of dollars.

There's Fury. I pick him up fondly. I remember him from Saturday mornings long ago. Fury—"The story of a horse and the boy who loved him." The boy's name was Joey. When I was nine, I wanted to marry Joey—but only so I could ride Fury!

Suppose that you have a friend who loves horses. Your friend would love to own a horse but lives in a city apartment. So you're sending your friend a plastic horse model as a birthday present. To go along with the gift, write a letter to your friend—from the horse's point of view. (Write the letter as if it's from the horse.) In your letter, use information from the article "Horse Dreams" and the story on page 169.

In your letter, be sure to explain

- who "you" are and where you come from
- some facts about horse models and the people who own them
- why you think your friend will (or will not) enjoy collecting horse models as a hobby

This question asks you to do several things. You need to *explain* some things about horse models. You need to give some *facts and details* about horse models and the people who own them. You need to *persuade* someone to share your opinion about horse models. And you need to style your letter in a creative way, from the *point of view* of a toy horse. Think of all these things as you plan and organize your answer. You might want to start by separating the facts from the opinions that you gather from the story and the article.

Facts	Opinions
• There are many kinds of horse models.	• Kids who like horses enjoy playing with horse models.
• Lots of them are from old TV shows.	• Horse models are expensive.
• Breyer seems to be the best-known brand name.	• Breyers are "the way to go."
• Many models are from horses in books and movies.	
• Prices start at around $25.	

Think about your main idea, too. It might be something like one of these:

Collecting horse models is the next best thing to owning a horse. Or,

You probably won't want to start a collection because...

The next step is to write a draft of your letter. Then revise and edit it. Remember to proofread and check your writing for correct spelling, grammar, capitalization, and punctuation.

Here is a letter that was written to respond to the question. Notice that even though it is written from the horse's point of view, it contains all the important information about horse models that the question asks for. The main idea of this letter is to persuade someone that playing with horse models is more fun than just collecting them.

Happy birthday! My name is Hidalgo. You saw me in a movie not long ago. I know you love horses, so I think you will enjoy me. Kids who love horses have played with models like me for more than 50 years! There are adults who collect horse models. But playing with horse models and collecting them are two different things. Before you start a collection, there are a few things you should know.

I have a large family. Most of us are made by a company in New Jersey called Breyer®. When they first started, TV shows with horses in them were popular. A lot of my brothers and sisters were copied from those TV horses. One of my most popular brothers was called Buttermilk. He was a light tan color with a dark brown mane and tail. Kids who knew him from TV loved to play with him. Today, only adults remember who he was. Kids who own him today might not even know his name. And if they have him, their parents probably had to pay a lot of money for him.

See, that's the problem with being a collector's item. You start out as a toy, but you end up being a business. Take Buttermilk, for instance. Long ago, kids used to make up stories about him. They would have make-believe races with him. He was a lot of fun. Today, he might be on display in a show. He might be too valuable to play with. I don't know how Buttermilk feels about that. But it would make me feel sad.

So please play with me. Find some friends who like playing with plastic horse models, too. You can brag about the brain space between my ears if you like. It won't embarrass me. And if you like me, you might want to get some of my brothers and sisters. Some of them come from your favorite horse books and movies. But please, don't think of me as a brand name! My name is Hidalgo. I'm not a collector's item. I'm a horse.

Test Yourself

In Lesson 23, you read two poems about leaves in fall. Now read an article about the science of autumn leaves and answer the question that follows.

Mysteries of Autumn
by Einar F. Klamst

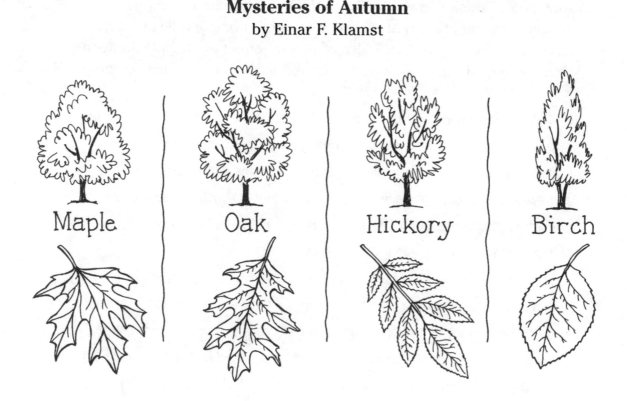

Maple   Oak   Hickory   Birch

The maples are usually the first to turn. They may start showing yellow and red soon after school begins. Then the oaks and hickories join the fashion parade. By mid-October the forests are in full display. Last to turn are the birches. They may still be putting on a show as Thanksgiving nears. By then, other trees are bare.

The beauty of autumn leaves is one of the pleasures of the season. It's one of the first things children in school study about nature. Songs and poems have been written about leaves changing colors. City people travel to the country in autumn for the best views. They bring their cameras. Artists set up their easels and paint the scenery.

But why do leaves turn bright colors just before they fall? Oh, sure—it has to do with chemicals in the leaves. Science has known this for some time. These colorful chemicals are called *pigments*. But what purpose do they serve? Nature would not have made them just so people could say "How pretty!" They must help the trees in some way.

Just what fall colors do for the trees has long been a mystery. Now science is solving it. It seems that different colors do different jobs!

Take yellow, for instance. Yellow pigments are actually present in leaves all summer. They help combine energy from sunlight with material from soil, water, and air. This process makes food for the tree to grow on. You don't notice the yellow in summer because the green pigment is so much brighter. In fall, though, the food-making process shuts down. The trees recycle energy from the green pigment. They take it out of the leaves and store it in the bark. When the green is gone, the leaves look yellow. But the color was there all along.

Red and purple pigments were a bigger mystery. They have nothing to do with helping trees grow. They are produced only in fall. It costs the trees a lot of energy to make them. It's as though the trees are paying for them. So why would tree leaves make red or purple pigments?

It seems that red pigments protect leaves from the sun. In autumn, a tree is trying to store away all the food-making materials before winter begins. Bright sunny days and cold nights can make leaves fall before this happens. Then the trees will not be as strong. But the red color acts as a kind of sunscreen! It keeps the leaves from falling until the process is complete.

Scientists started studying fall colors because they were curious. But then they discovered that leaf pigments can show how healthy a tree is. It's like taking a person's temperature. An unusually bright red or purple may show that a tree is sick. The tree may produce the pigment for protection against disease. And what's true for a tree may be true for a forest. A show of color may be a sign of climate change or pollution.

Fall colors are beautiful. But an especially beautiful fall may mean that all is not well in the woods.

Suppose that your town or city is planning a Fall Festival. It is an autumn of unusually brilliant reds and purples. You have been asked to write an essay celebrating the season. Write it from the point of view of both a scientist and someone who admires nature's beauty.

In your essay, be sure to include

- thoughts about why people celebrate autumn

- a comparison and contrast of fall colors from both points of view

- ideas from both the poems and the article

Use the space below for prewriting. Read the question again and make notes about how to answer it. You might want to use a graphic organizer for your ideas. Next, write your draft on the following page. Remember to revise, edit, and proofread your essay. Check your writing for correct spelling, grammar, capitalization, and punctuation. Then write your final answer on a separate sheet of paper.

Use the space below to write your draft.